Published by

Onyourgates

6539 Noffke Dr.
Caledonia, Michigan 49316
Marie@onyourgates.com
(616) 893-4880
www.onyourgates.com

The 30 Second Bible

By Steven Elzinga, edited Claudia Mindes

Just 30 seconds a day could change your life and the lives of those around you.

1. 30 seconds is all you need to express your love to those close to you.
2. 30 seconds is all you need to engage in an act of kindness to a stranger.
3. 30 seconds is all you need to bless your children or a friend.
4. 30 seconds is all you need to conceive a child that will be loved and cherished.
5. 30 seconds is all you need to decide to see a person or situation in a positive light.
6. 30 seconds is all you need to ask a friend for help.
7. 30 seconds is all you need to admit your shortcomings and faults.
8. 30 seconds is all you need to encourage someone who needs a lift.
9. 30 seconds is all you need to look up to the heavens just to wonder.
10. 30 seconds is all you need to say hello to one person you have never said hello to before.
11. 30 seconds is all you need to express your thanks, your sorrow, and your needs

to the God of the Bible.

12. 30 seconds is all you need to be encouraged, challenged, comforted, and inspired by the Word of God.

This is the 30 Second Bible!

So do you have 30 seconds?

Why not pick a few of these ideas or add one or two of your own—things you could do 30 seconds a day—things that just might change your life and the lives of those around you?

What is the 30 Second Bible and why should you bother reading it?

The #1 criticism of the Bible by those who do not read it on a daily basis is that the Bible is boring and irrelevant. Well, it can be.

The Bible was written in three different ancient languages, thousands of years ago by and for people who were from wildly different cultures than our own. Without a basic understanding of the life and times of Biblical events, most people struggle to get something out of it.

But, although some of the Bible may be difficult to understand, much of the Bible is very understandable and surprisingly relevant to our lives and time.

The 30 Second Bible presents the Word of God in small, clear, understandable verses. Then, to help apply these verses to your life, the 30 Second Bible adds a few guiding thoughts, capped off with a question that will help you reflect throughout your day on what you have read. All of this in 30 seconds.

You'll be surprised at how often the verses you read each day fit exactly with what you are facing and experiencing.

If the God of the Bible is not real, all you will lose is 30 seconds.

If the God of the Bible is real, 30 seconds could change your life and the lives of those who are dear to you.

There are at least four different ways to engage the 30 Second Bible:

1. **Topically.** Find the topic that interests you in the table of contents and read the 7 entries on that topic.

2. **Daily.** There are 365 entries in the 30 Second Bible—one per day. You can start reading any time during the year.

3. **Sequentially.** Start reading the first verse, thought, and question, and read as much or little of the others as you have time for—just like any book you might read.

4. **Randomly.** Turn to any page in the 30 Second Bible and read whichever verse or verses you want.

Contents

Note: Holy Week is found on pages 30 & 31. The Christmas Season is found on pages 102 through 111.

Notes:

***Job 14:1,2** Man who is born of woman is of few days and full of trouble. He comes forth like a flower and fades away; He flees like a shadow and does not continue. (NKJV)*

Your life will be short and, if you haven't figured it out yet, full of trouble. The trouble will keep you busy. But in the end, what will you do with the few days you have on this earth?

***Matthew 7:7** Ask, and it will be given to you; seek, and you will find; knock, and it will be opened to you. (NIV)*

What are you waiting for? Ask, seek, knock. What do you need to ask God for? What are you seeking at this time in your life? What doors do you need to knock on?

***Luke 9:62** Jesus said, "No procrastination. No backward looks. You can't put God's kingdom off till tomorrow. Seize the day." (The Message)*

If God is real, why would anyone ignore Him? If God is busy building His kingdom, why would anyone not want to be a part of that? How are you seizing the Kingdom of God?

***James 4:13-15** Now listen, you who say, "Today or tomorrow we will go to this or that city, spend a year there, carry on business and make money." Why, you do not even know what will happen tomorrow. What is your life? You are a mist that appears for a little while and then vanishes. Instead, you ought to say, "If it is the Lord's will,*

Notes:

we will live and do this or that." (NIV)

Seize the day. Yes. But remember to whom the day belongs. How can you both seize the day and give it to God?

Psalm 40:1 I waited patiently for the Lord; he turned to me and heard my cry. He lifted me out of the slimy pit, out of the mud and mire; he set my feet on a rock and gave me a firm place to stand. He put a new song in my mouth, a hymn of praise to our God. (NIV)

Perhaps you have been singing the blues for some time now. God hears you and He will put a new song in your mouth. At this point in your life, what song speaks most to you?

Psalm 118:23-25 This is the day that the Lord has made; let us rejoice and be glad in it. (ESV)

This very day was carefully, purposefully and wonderfully prepared for you by the God of the universe. What will you do with it?

Proverbs 30:25 Ants—they aren't strong, but they store up food all summer. (NLT)

Success does not always go to the big and strong. Often it goes to those who work at it. There are things that you must do today. Don't put them off. Make a "to do" list. Make this "to do" list your prayer list. Then act. Do something. What have you been procrastinating on?

Notes:

Philippians 4:13 I can do everything through Christ, who gives me strength. (NLT)

You have dreams. God has dreams for you. Be a risk-taker for God's kingdom and He will make your dreams come true. What is your spiritual dream?

Ephesians 3:20 Now all glory to God, who is able, through his mighty power at work within us, to accomplish infinitely more than we might ask or think. (NLT)

You have a spiritual dream. But whatever it is, God's dream for you is beyond your own. What do you think God's spiritual dream is for you?

Luke 6:38 Give, and you will receive. Your gift will return to you in full—pressed down, shaken together to make room for more, running over, and poured into your lap. The amount you give will determine the amount you get back. (NLT)

You want to give. People say it's good to give. You have been on the receiving end of others' giving. But it is just so counter-intuitive. You have needs of your own and if you give you might end up with even more needs. And then where will you be? Giving is risky. That's why it's so much fun! How can you join in on the fun of risky giving?

Philippians 4:13 I can do everything through Him (Christ) who gives me strength. (NIV)

God will provide you with tremendous opportunities to do great things. What opportunities does God seem to

Notes:

be putting before you?

1 Corinthians 15:58 ***My dear friends, stand firm and don't be shaken. Always keep busy working for the Lord. You know that everything you do for him is worthwhile. (CEV)***

If you are a christian you are on the winning team. It's a done deal. You have nothing to lose. What would you attempt to do if you knew you couldn't fail?

2 Timothy 1:7a God did not give us a spirit of timidity. (NIV)

Go out on a limb today. "But," you ask, "what if the wind blows and the branch I am depending on breaks?" Yes, that could happen. And you could just sit at the trunk of the tree. It's safe there. Still, go out on a limb today. Why? That's where the fruit is. When in your life have you been timid? When has God given you courage?

Jeremiah 29:11 "For I know the plans I have for you," declares the Lord, "plans to prosper you and not to harm you, plans to give you hope and a future...." (NIV)

God has a special plan for you! Never forget it. Seek it. Pray for it. Follow it. Enjoy it. How have you seen God's plan so far in your life?

Notes:

Proverbs 12:24 Work hard and become a leader; be lazy and become a slave. (NLT)

A leader? You? Yes, you. If you have an influence on anyone, then you're a leader. What can you do today to become a better leader?

Hebrews 13:7 Remember your leaders who first taught you the word of God. Think of all the good that has come from their lives, and trust the Lord as they do. (NLT)

Write down the names of people who have made a big difference in your life. What about them do you want to imitate?

John 15:16 You did not choose me, but I chose you and appointed you to go and bear fruit—fruit that will last. (NIV)

If you have two children and they grow up, get married, and have two children, and this pattern continues, in 400 years you will have one million people in your family tree. What aspects of you will remain in them?

Proverbs 22:6 Teach your children to choose the right path, and when they are older, they will remain upon it. (NLT)

What spiritual legacy will you leave your family? Your friends? Your world?

Notes:

1 Peter 5:3 *Don't lord it over the people assigned to your care, but lead them by your own good example. (NLT)*

You may not feel like a leader, but that is what God is making you to be. God wants to use you to help others. That's what being a leader is. You can help others by your good example. Who is learning from your example? What are they learning?

1 Thessalonians 5:14 *And we urge you, brothers, warn those who are idle, encourage the timid, help the weak, be patient with everyone. (NIV)*

You get the idea from this verse that we are supposed to take a real interest in the lives of the people around us. Who in your life needs a warning, a word of encouragement, or some help?

Philippians 4:9 *Whatever you have learned or received or heard from me, or seen in me—put it into practice. And the God of peace will be with you. (NIV)*

If you are a Christian, you have been called to follow Christ's example. By following His example you will, in return, set an example for others to follow. What of your lifestyle is worth following?

Notes:

Ephesians 6:10 A final word: Be strong in the Lord and in his mighty power. (NLT)

You can't do it. You feel like giving up. You are tired and worn out. You can't do it, but God can do it through you. God's mighty power is within you. Where in your life have you experienced God's power? Where in your life do you need God's power?

2 Chronicles 20:17 You will not have to fight this battle. Take up your positions; stand firm and see the deliverance the LORD will give you, O Judah and Jerusalem. Do not be afraid; do not be discouraged. Go out to face them tomorrow, and the LORD will be with you. (NIV)

You have some battles on your hands. Even though God promises to fight your battles, He still calls you out. What battles have you had to fight lately?

Ephesians 3:16 I pray that from his glorious, unlimited resources he (Jesus) will give you mighty inner strength through his Holy Spirit. (NLT)

When it comes down to it, who you are and what you do come from the inside. Specifically ask Jesus today to fill the treasure chest of your soul with His unlimited resources. What are you facing today that will require strength on the inside?

Psalm 46:1,2 God is our refuge and strength, an ever-present help in trouble. Therefore we will not fear, though the earth give way and the mountains fall into the heart of the sea. (NIV)

No matter what disasters have happened to you, no matter what fearful events lay before you, God is ever-present. When, in the midst of trouble, have you felt the presence of God?

Isaiah 33:2 O Lord, be gracious to us; we long for you. Be our strength every morning, our salvation in time of distress. (NIV)

Perhaps you have many things planned for your day. You can attempt to carry out your plans on your own strength or on God's strength. Is God one of the first things you think of in the morning? Why or why not?

2 Corinthians 4:8 We are hard pressed on every side, but not crushed; perplexed, but not in despair .... (NIV)

Hard pressed on every side—at work, at home, from family, from friends, from strangers. Perplexed—expectations not met, promises made to you and then broken, friendships inexplicably ended. But strangely, you are not crushed and not in despair. It must be God's strength. How does this describe your circumstances lately?

Psalm 73:26 My flesh and my heart may fail, but God is the strength of my heart and my portion forever. (NIV)

If this is your testimony, what can stand in your way?

Notes:

Notes:

Proverbs 10:5 A wise youth harvests in the summer, but one who sleeps during harvest is a disgrace. (NLT)

This is the one chance you have to live, laugh, cry, work, try, accomplish, dream, and perform. Grab this day. Seize it. Enjoy it. Celebrate it. Don't waste it. What "harvest" opportunities do you see before you?

2 Samuel 6:14 David, wearing a linen ephod, danced before the LORD with all his might. (NIV)

Dancing? Working? Worshiping? Studying? Singing? Playing? What are you doing before the Lord with all your might?

2 Chronicles 31:20,21 Thus Hezekiah ... did what was good and right and faithful before the Lord his God. And every work that he undertook in the service of the house of God and in accordance with the law and the commandments, seeking his God, he did with all his heart, and prospered. (ESV)

Sounds like a good way to live. How might this be said of you at the end of your life?

Romans 12:11 Never be lacking in zeal, but keep your spiritual fervor, serving the Lord. (NIV)

Lacking ambition lately? No enthusiasm? Sleepy in the middle of the day? Try serving the Lord. Find something that needs doing in God's kingdom and do it! See what happens. What could you do?

Notes:

1 Thessalonians 5:19 Do not put out the Spirit's fire. (NIV)

To wake up every morning with a passion for God and His Word, and a passion for His plan for your life and for God's plan for your family; to greet every morning with a passion for the success of God's kingdom, the church you attend, and the mission of reaching people for Christ—this is the Spirit's desire for you every morning. How are you fanning the Spirit's fire?

1 Corinthians 9:24 Don't you realize that in a race everyone runs, but only one person gets the prize? So run to win! (NLT)

Today is one more chance to run for the winning team. Enjoy the race. If your heart does not beat strongly for the cause of Christ, what does it beat strongly for? What are you running hard for?

Psalm 86:11 Teach me your way, O LORD, and I will walk in your truth; give me an undivided heart, that I may fear your name. (NIV)

You want God in your life. You want to walk in His way. You want to live by His truth. But you also want to walk in your own way and live by your own truth. How "sold out" are you in your walk with the Lord?

Notes:

Matthew 11:12 From the days of John the Baptist until now, the Kingdom of God has been forcefully advancing, and forceful men lay hold of it. (NIV)

Christianity is not a sit-back religion. Stand up and do something for God today. How are you advancing the kingdom of God?

Joshua 1:9 Have I not commanded you? Be strong and courageous. Do not be terrified; do not be discouraged, for the LORD your God will be with you wherever you go. (NIV)

Wow! What a promise. This is a verse worth memorizing. What situations are you going to face today that just may require some boldness on your part?

Psalm 27:1 The Lord is my light and my salvation—whom shall I fear? The Lord is the stronghold of my life—of whom shall I be afraid? (NIV)

As you attempt to make things happen today, be bold. Whom do you fear? What do you fear?

Psalm 138:3 When I called, you answered me; you made me bold and stouthearted. (NIV)

"Lord, give me opportunities today that will require boldness on my part—and then give me the boldness to respond to whatever opportunities come my way." Are you bold enough to pray this prayer?

Notes:

Psalm 18:1 The LORD is my rock, my fortress and my deliverer; my God is my rock, in whom I take refuge. He is my shield and the horn of my salvation, my stronghold. (NIV)

Maybe your day looks like a minefield—there are people and events that could blow up in your face. Follow the Lord in all you do and he will guide you through. What potential minefields do you face today?

Philippians 1:20 For I fully expect and hope that I will never be ashamed, but that I will continue to be bold for Christ, as I have been in the past. And I trust that my life will bring honor to Christ, whether I live or die. (NLT)

To be bold for something that is worth dying for—that is true living. How can you be bold for Christ today? Or, what would it take for you to be bold for Christ today?

Luke 18:38,39 [A blind man] called out, "Jesus, Son of David, have mercy on me!" Those who led the way rebuked him and told him to be quiet, but he shouted all the more, "Son of David, have mercy on me!" (NIV)

Sometimes asking for help is more about boldness than weakness. Where in your life do you need to be bold in asking for help?

Notes:

Psalm 90:12 Teach us to number our days aright, that we may gain a heart of wisdom. (NIV)

Spend a little time looking back at what you have done or not done, and then look forward to what you might yet do. With a little reflecting or "numbering," you may gain the wisdom to make the most of the precious time you have on this earth. What does this verse mean to you?

Proverbs 13:20 He who walks with the wise grows wise, but a companion of fools suffers harm. (NIV)

Wisdom is more about who you associate with than how much you know. So how wise are you? How is your wisdom evidenced in the friends you have?

Proverbs 24:27 Finish your outdoor work and get your fields ready; after that, build your house. (NIV)

If you have food but no house, at least you don't starve to death. It's about priorities. Do what is most important first. If you made a list of your priorities for this day, what would that list look like?

Psalm 39:6 Man is a mere phantom as he goes to and from: he bustles about, but only in vain; he heaps up wealth, not knowing who will get it. (NIV)

No one at the end of life wishes they had acquired more possessions. What do you think most people wish for at the end of life?

Notes:

Proverbs 10:8 If you have good sense, you will listen and obey; if all you do is talk, you will destroy yourself. (CEV)

Usually the person doing all the talking thinks he or she is the smart one. Perhaps it's just the other way around. When, latel,y should you have just listened and obeyed rather than talked?

Proverbs 1:7 Respect and obey the Lord! This is the beginning of knowledge. Only a fool rejects wisdom and good advice. (CEV)

Life is not so much about what you know but with whom you have a relationship. You can be the smartest person on earth but if you don't know God, the creator of the earth, what do you really know? How is God the beginning of wisdom?

Luke 10:21 At that time Jesus, full of joy through the Holy Spirit, said, "I praise you, Father, Lord of heaven and earth, because you have hidden these things from the wise and learned, and revealed them to little children." (NIV)

Walking with God is not about how smart you are. He speaks and reveals His will and gives insight and revelations to whom He pleases. Has He revealed hidden things to you?

Notes:

1 Corinthians 4:7 What do you have that God hasn't given you? (NLT)

All that you have. All that you are. All that you will have. All that you will ever be. All is from God. How can you show your thanks for all that God has given you?

Philemon 1:4 I always thank my God as I remember you in my prayers. (NIV)

Think about some of the great people in your life—people that have helped you, that have believed in you, supported you, given you opportunities to grow as a child of God. Why not thank God for them today? Who are some of these great people in your life?

Proverbs 11:25 A generous man will prosper; he who refreshes others will himself be refreshed. (NIV)

The word misery comes from the word "miser." If you are a miser with your money, your affection, and your love, you will be miserable. Want to be prosperous? Be generous! On a scale of 1 to 10, rate how others see your generosity.

1 Thessalonians 5:18 Give thanks in all circumstances, for this is God's will for you in Christ Jesus. (NIV)

It may not be easy to give thanks today. But giving thanks when it's hard to give thanks is the perfect time to give thanks! You cannot be negative and be thankful at the same time. What things are you thankful for today?

Notes:

Psalm 13:6 I will sing to the LORD, for he has been good to me. (NIV)

He has, you know. He's been good to you. Not that your life has been easy. But in spite of all the ups and downs, you have it all: a life and a life to come. Oh, and a chance to give life to others. How has God been good to you today?

Psalm 30:11,12 You turned my wailing into dancing; you removed my sackcloth and clothed me with joy, that my heart may sing to you and not be silent. O LORD my God, I will give you thanks forever. (NIV)

What you thought was bad turned out good. What you thought was sad—through strange and unusual circumstances—made you glad. Give thanks for the turn-arounds in your life. What has turned for the good in your life lately?

Colossians 3:16 Let the word of Christ dwell in you richly as you teach and admonish one another with all wisdom, and as you sing psalms, hymns and spiritual songs with gratitude in your hearts to God. (NIV)

A good day. It starts with the Word. From the Word, we use God's wisdom as we interact with each other. Then there is singing. We end our day with gratitude. A good day. Was it?

Notes:

3 John 1:14 Peace be to you. The friends here send their greetings. Greet the friends there by name. (NIV)

You may remember a time when someone you only met once remembered you by name. It probably gave you a special feeling of importance and being loved. Do this for someone else today. Whom can you greet warmly today?

John 15:15 "I (Jesus) no longer call you servants, because a servant does not know his master's business. Instead, I have called you friends, for everything that I learned from my Father I have made known to you." (NIV)

God isn't interested in a superficial relationship with you. He wants to connect with you at the deepest of all levels—friendship. How is your friendship with the Lord these days?

Proverbs 27:19 As a face is reflected in water, so the heart reflects the real person. (NLT)

You can have friends that either bring you down or build you up. The choice is yours. Choose the building-up kind. Based on the friends you spend time with, who are you?

Ecclesiastes 4:9,10 Two people are better off than one, for they can help each other succeed. If one person falls, the other can reach out and help. But someone who falls alone is in real trouble. (NLT)

It takes two to have a friendship. If you have a

friend, consider yourself blessed. If you do not have a close friend, consider being a friend to someone who needs one. Do you have many real friends? Why or why not?

Proverbs 17:17 A friend loves at all times, and a brother is born for adversity. (NIV)

You find out who your friends are when things are not going well. Your friends are the ones who are still by your side. Do you have friends like that? Are you a friend like that?

Proverbs 27:6 Wounds from a friend can be trusted, but an enemy multiplies kisses. (NIV)

Perhaps a friend has said some hard words to your face—words that spoke the truth but words that hurt. Be thankful. Your enemies speak kind words to your face but lies behind your back. How are you at receiving "words" from a friend?

Psalm 1:1 Blessed is the one who does not walk in step with the wicked or stand in the way that sinners take or sit in the company of mockers ... (NIV)

Your friends, the people you associate with the most, will have more influence over your thoughts and ways than you realize. Choose your friends wisely. Who are your best friends? Do they help you in your walk with God or do they more often cause you to stumble?

Notes:

Notes:

Romans 1:17 ***For in the gospel a righteousness from God is revealed, a righteousness that is by faith from first to last, just as it is written: "The righteous will live by faith." (NIV)***

On the night before All Saints Day which was called "All Hallows Eve," Martin Luther nailed 95 discussion points on the door of the Wittenberg church in Germany. This verse played a key role in his thinking. What do you think of it?

Isaiah 7:9b ***If you do not stand firm in your faith, you will not stand at all. (NIV)***

Your faith in God will give you the strength to stand when the influences around you seek to push you over. So what will it be today—pushover or firm stander?

Ephesians 3:16,17a ***I pray that out of his glorious riches he may strengthen you with power through his Spirit in your inner being, so that Christ may dwell in your hearts through faith. (NIV)***

How do you feel today? Confident? Bold? Strong? Fearful? Insignificant? Weak? God's Spirit is His gift to you today. A Spirit of power and strength. What do you think it means to let Christ dwell in your heart through faith?

Ephesians 2:8,9 ***For it is by grace you have been saved, through faith—and this not from yourselves, it is the gift of God—not by works, so that no one can boast. (NIV)***

What can you do today to make God love you?

Notes:

Nothing! What can you do today to get God to save you? Nothing! Oh, but you must have faith. Yes. But even faith is a gift. Have you accepted the gift of faith from God?

1 Thessalonians 5:23,24 ***Now may the God of peace make you holy in every way, and may your whole spirit and soul and body be kept blameless until our Lord Jesus Christ comes again. God will make this happen, for he who calls you is faithful. (NLT)***

God has started something special in your life. He will be faithful to complete what He has begun. How have you seen God working in your life?

2 Corinthians 5:7 ***We live by faith, not by sight. (NIV)***

Maybe you are struggling to believe in a God you cannot see. Faith is a struggle. If there is a struggle going on within you, then there is faith. And faith is all you need. What doubts do you struggle with? How has your faith become more certain?

1 Samuel 17:4 ***A champion named Goliath, who was from Gath, came out of the Philistine camp. He was over nine feet tall. (NIV)***

Perhaps there are some threatening giants in your life—giants that make you and your faith feel small, helpless, and vulnerable. Pick up your slingshot, a couple of stones, and what faith you have in God, and face them. What "giants" threaten your life and faith?

Notes:

Joshua 1:9 ***Be strong and courageous. Do not be terrified; do not be discouraged, for the Lord your God will be with you wherever you go. (NIV)***

Go for it today. You are strong! You are courageous! You are not terrified! You are not discouraged! Why? Because God is with you today! What would you attempt to do if you knew God was behind you?

Psalm 32:7 ***For you are my hiding place; you protect me from trouble. You surround me with songs of victory. (NLT)***

Ever feel like a loser? Trouble will make you feel that way. God is a winner and you are on His team. When in your life were you on a winning team? What experience in your life made you feel like you were on God's winning team?

Joshua 1:7 ***Be strong and very courageous. Be careful to obey all the law my servant Moses gave you; do not turn from it to the right or to the left, that you may be successful wherever you go. (NIV)***

Not feeling strong today? Not very courageous? Perfect. This verse is for you. Of course there is a catch. You must do things God's way. Then you will be a success. What things are you facing today that will require strength and courage?

Proverbs 31:8 ***Speak up for those who cannot speak for themselves, for the rights of all who are destitute. (NIV)***

Notes:

There is someone you know; someone in your class, or at work, or in your neighborhood; someone that isn't quite right, or is a bit different; someone picked on; someone not strong enough to stand up for themselves. What can you do today to speak up for this person?

Daniel 3:17,18 "If we are thrown into the blazing furnace, the God we serve is able to save us from it, and he will rescue us from your hand, O king. But even if he does not, we want you to know, O king, that we will not serve your gods or worship the image of gold you have set up." (NIV)

Trusting in God no matter what! Can you imagine how brave you could be if you had this attitude?

Isaiah 40:31 But they that wait upon the Lord shall renew their strength; they shall mount up with wings as eagles; they shall run, and not be weary; and they shall walk, and not faint. (KJV)

Ever have the dream where you can fly? You can. Trust God for the strength and courage to fly over your problems. Where in your life do you need God's strength?

Psalm 94:18 When I said, "My foot is slipping," your love, O Lord, supported me. (NIV)

You have been trying to do the right thing but there is a lot of pressure from friends, co-workers, and perhaps even your own desire to get ahead - pressure to cave in. Take courage. God Himself will support you. Where is your foot slipping these days?

Notes:

Luke 23:33,34 When they came to the place called the Skull, there they crucified him, along with the criminals—one on his right, the other on his left. Jesus said, "Father, forgive them, for they do not know what they are doing." (NIV)

Jesus spoke only seven words or phrases during the most important event in history and the first word was about forgiveness. Have you received it? Who do you need to give it to?

Luke 23:43 Jesus answered him, "I tell you the truth, today you will be with me in paradise." (NIV)

Jesus' second word from the cross was to a thief who deserved to die on a cross but who would live forever in heaven, all because he turned to Jesus for help at the end. Why is it smart not to wait until the very end to make the decision to accept Christ?

John 19:26,27 When Jesus saw his mother there, and the disciple whom he loved standing nearby, he said to his mother, "Dear woman, here is your son," and to the disciple, "Here is your mother." From that time on, this disciple took her into his home. (NIV)

Jesus' third word from the cross was about His concern for His mother—His earthly family. How important is family to you?

Mark 15:34 And at the ninth hour Jesus cried out in a loud voice, "Eloi, Eloi, lama sabachthani?"—which means, "My God, my God, why have you forsaken me?" (NIV)

Notes:

Jesus' fourth word on the cross was perhaps His most painful. He was rejected by His own Father. But it had to happen. He was rejected in our place so that we will be forever accepted. When have you felt the sting of rejection?

John 19:28,29 Later, knowing that all was now completed, and so that the Scripture would be fulfilled, Jesus said, "I am thirsty." A jar of wine vinegar was there, so they soaked a sponge in it, put the sponge on a stalk of the hyssop plant, and lifted it to Jesus' lips. (NIV)

Jesus' fifth word on the cross has an Old Testament connection. Look it up. Exodus 12:22. What do you think the connection means?

John 19:30 When he had received the drink, Jesus said, "It is finished." (NIV)

Notice Jesus did not say that He was finished. He said it was finished. The devil was finished. The payment for sin was finished. The reign of death was finished. The reign of sin in your life is finished. What has Jesus finished in your life?

Luke 23:46 Jesus called out with a loud voice, "Father, into your hands I commit my spirit." When he had said this, he breathed his last. (NIV)

One day you will give up your last breath. But in that moment you will be in the hands of God the Father—waiting your resurrection day.

Notes:

Romans 5:4 We can rejoice, too, when we run into problems and trials, for we know that they help us develop endurance. And endurance develops strength of character, and character strengthens our confident hope of salvation. (NLT)

Do you want to be strong and steady in your faith and hope? Pray for something today that will require your endurance. What in life would test your ability to endure?

James 1:3 When your faith is tested, your endurance has a chance to grow. (NLT)

You never really know what it is you stand for until someone or something tries to push you over. You never really know what it is you believe until what you believe costs you something. Thank God for the tests in your life. How has your faith been tested? How did you do in the test?

Hebrews 12:1 Therefore, since we are surrounded by such a great cloud of witnesses, let us throw off everything that hinders and the sin that so easily entangles, and let us run with perseverance the race marked out for us. (NIV)

Listen. Do you hear them? There is a crowd cheering you on when you feel like giving up. Who are the "fans" in your life who inspire you?

2 Corinthians 4:9 In times of trouble, God is with us, and when we are knocked down, we get up again. (CEV)

Notes:

When you were learning how to walk, you fell down hundreds of times. But, you got up and tried again, and eventually you learned how to walk. In the same way, you can overcome whatever is knocking you down now because God is ready to help you. What is knocking you down lately? How is God lifting you up?

1 Corinthians 15:58 So, my dear brothers and sisters, be strong and immovable. Always work enthusiastically for the Lord, for you know that nothing you do for the Lord is ever useless. (NLT)

You may feel like it's not worth it today. God knows your efforts and struggles. Don't lose heart! Everything you do for the Lord is worth it. When was the last time you felt like giving up?

2 Corinthians 4:17 For our light and momentary troubles are achieving for us an eternal glory that far outweighs them all. (NIV)

Sometimes being a Christian means you will encounter more trouble, not less. But suffering trouble for the sake of your relationship with God pays off beyond your wildest dreams. What trouble have you experienced because of your faith?

Romans 8:17 Since we are his children, we will share his treasures—for everything God gives to his Son, Christ, is ours, too. But if we are to share his glory, we must also share his suffering. (NLT)

If you are in God's family, you can count on suffering. If you are in God's family, you can also count on winning and sharing in the glory. How goes the battle?

Notes:

Psalm 130:3,4 If you, O LORD, kept a record of sins, O Lord, who could stand? But with you there is forgiveness; therefore you are feared. (NIV)

Can you imagine a record book filled with your every misspoken word, misdeed, evil thought, and missed opportunity for doing good? God's forgiveness is like the delete button on a computer. Have you taken advantage of the delete button lately?

Psalm 103:10 He does not treat us as our sins deserve or repay us according to our iniquities. (NIV)

Life is not fair. People say lies about you. People take advantage of you. People treat you poorly. Life is not fair. God sent His Son to die on the cross in your place. Life is not fair. Thank God. Why do you think Jesus died in your place?

Romans 15:7 Accept one another, then, just as Christ accepted you, in order to bring praise to God. (NIV)

There is nothing you can do to make God love you more than He does right now. He accepts you just the way you are. Do the same for someone else today. Who in your life needs to feel accepted? How can you help?

1 Peter 2:24 He himself (Jesus) bore our sins in his body on the tree (the cross), that we might die to sin and live to righteousness. By his wounds you have been healed. (ESV)

Sin is a debt. Debts must be paid. Even if the one to whom the debt is owed decides to forgive the debt, the debt must still be paid. This is what Jesus did for us on the cross. What sins do you want Jesus to forgive for you?

Isaiah 53:6 We all, like sheep, have gone astray, each of us has turned to his own way; and the LORD has laid on him the iniquity of us all. (NIV)

Left on our own, we tend to go the wrong way and end up hurting, not only ourselves, but others as well. Jesus not only forgives us but also leads us in the right way. Where have you been tempted to wander off?

Proverbs 10:12 Hatred stirs up trouble; love overlooks the wrongs that others do. (CEV)

They let you down. They betrayed you. They were insensitive to your needs. They didn't follow through with their part. They said hurtful, untrue words about you. You have every right to be angry at them. You could go with that anger and make some trouble or, by the grace of God, you could let it go. Which are you going with today?

Galatians 2:20 I have been crucified with Christ; and it is no longer I who live, but Christ lives in me; and the [life] I now live in the flesh I live by faith in the Son of God, who loved me, and delivered Himself up for me. (NASB)

When you feel overwhelmed and everything is out of control, remember you live by faith. Jesus lives in you. Jesus Christ loves you and is your salvation. Do you trust Him? When did you first trust Him?

Notes:

Notes:

Proverbs 20:5 The purposes of a man's heart are deep waters, but a man of understanding draws them out. (NIV)

Look for good advice today from a friend, your family, and God's Word. How open are you to others' advice?

Isaiah 50:4b He wakens me morning by morning, wakens my ear to listen like one being taught. (NIV)

Getting up can be a real chore. But picture this—God is waking you each morning. He wants you awake so you can hear all He has to say. Each morning He whispers in your ear, "Good morning, my child. I love you, and I'll be with you through this day." How do you wake up in the morning? How teachable are you?

Job 8:10 But those who came before us will teach you. They will teach you the wisdom of old. (NLV)

Don't go at it alone. Why repeat the mistakes of the past? If you know some godly mentors, listen to them. If you don't know any godly mentors, find some. Who have been some of the godly mentors in your life?

Psalm 25:4,5a Show me your ways, O Lord, teach me your paths; guide me in your truth and teach me, for you are God my Savior, and my hope is in you all day long. (NIV)

Life is a journey. There is a destination to this journey. Why not stop a moment and get some directions? How does God show you the way?

Notes:

Psalm 119:105 Your word is a lamp to guide my feet and a light for my path. (NLT)

God wants you to have a happy, successful life. As you read a little bit of the Bible each day, the path of life becomes a little bit easier to find. How has the Word of God helped you find your way recently?

Proverbs 15:31,32 If you listen to constructive criticism, you will be at home among the wise. If you reject discipline, you only harm yourself; but if you listen to correction, you grow in understanding. (NLT)

To desire growth is to admit you are not where you want to be. To admit you are not where you want to be is to be self-critical. Why not get the opinions of others as well? This is constructive criticism. How do you handle criticism?

Romans 15:4 For everything that was written in the past was written to teach us, so that through endurance and the encouragement of the Scriptures we might have hope. (NIV)

The Bible is a record book of God's dealings with His people in the past. If you want to know how God might deal with you, you might want to keep reading it. What have you read in the Bible lately that has spoken to you?

Notes:

***Psalm 46:10* Be still, and know that I am God; I will be exalted among the nations, I will be exalted in the earth. (NIV)**

Find a quiet place today—away from your phone, your iPod, your computer, your television—and just listen to the silence. Did God show up?

***Isaiah 40:26* Lift your eyes and look to the heavens: Who created all these? He who brings out the starry host one by one, and calls them each by name. Because of his great power and mighty strength, not one of them is missing. (NIV)**

The same God that created and named each star is the God who created and named you. Look at the night sky tonight. How does looking at the stars make you feel?

***Psalm 90:4* For a thousand years in your sight are like a day that has just gone by, or like a watch in the night. (NIV)**

Perhaps what is happening to you lately does not make much sense to you. Sometimes it's hard to see God's plan in your life. Maybe it's because His plan covers many generations, and your part in that plan is just a small part of something much larger. How does this realization make you feel?

***Psalm 144:4* Man is like a breath; his days are like a fleeting shadow. (NIV)**

Life is short, then you die. But there is more: then comes eternal life! So why are you so worried about the things that you must do today?

Ecclesiastes 1:11 There is no remembrance of men of old, and even those who are yet to come will not be remembered by those who follow. (NIV)

You are here today but soon—10, 20, 70 years from now—you will be gone. Soon after that, even the memory of you in those that follow you will be gone. But God will never forget you. How long do you think you will be remembered after you die?

Luke 4:42 At daybreak Jesus went out to a solitary place. (NIV)

Jesus needed to be alone—to recharge, refocus, reestablish His intimate relationship with His Father. If Jesus needed this, what makes you think you can get by without it? Where might your solitary place be? When can you go there?

Jeremiah 10:12,13 God made the earth by his power; he founded the world by his wisdom and stretched out the heavens by his understanding. When he thunders, the waters in the heavens roar; he makes clouds rise from the ends of the earth. He sends lightning with the rain and brings out the wind from his storehouses. (NIV)

This same awesome God wants to walk with you today. How will knowing that God walks with you make a difference?

Notes:

Notes:

2 Thessalonians 1:11,12 So we keep on praying for you, asking our God to enable you to live a life worthy of his call. May he give you the power to accomplish all the good things your faith prompts you to do. Then the name of our Lord Jesus will be honored because of the way you live, and you will be honored along with him. (NLT)

This is our prayer for you. Pray this prayer for others.

Proverbs 3:9,10 Honor the Lord with your wealth and with the best part of everything you produce. Then he will fill your barns with grain, and your vats will overflow with good wine. (NLT)

The key word here is "honor." Success in life is really about honor and respect. These two qualities require humility. Humility comes when you realize that all you have ultimately comes from God and is His. How are you honoring God with the best of all you have?

1 Peter 5:6 So humble yourselves under the mighty power of God, and at the right time he will lift you up in honor. (NLV)

You want honor? You want respect? It will come to you. Maybe not as quickly as you would like. Wait for it. Follow God's ways. Trust in Him. It will come. Why is respect and honor so important?

Psalm 122:1 I rejoiced with those who said to me, "Let us go to the house of the LORD." (NIV)

An invitation to a friend's house is an honor and a privilege. How much more when the friend is God

Notes:

Himself? And we get to be the ones doing the inviting! Who can you invite to church this Sunday?

Revelation 4:8 Each of the four living creatures had six wings and was covered with eyes all around, even under his wings. Day and night they never stop saying: "Holy, holy, holy is the Lord God Almighty, who was, and is, and is to come." (NIV)

God wants to be your friend but He is still a Holy God. He wants to walk with you in your ordinary up and down life, but He is still the Lord God Almighty. Give Him the honor due His name. What does it mean to you that God is Holy?

1 Thessalonians 5:12 Honor those who are your leaders in the Lord's work. (NLT)

Perhaps there are people whom God has placed in your life as spiritual leaders or mentors. Put some of these people in your prayers today. Are you being teachable to their counsel?

Exodus 20:12 Honor your father and your mother, so that you may live long in the land the Lord your God is giving you. (NIV)

God created the first man. And then the first woman came from that man. But every man and woman since has come from a woman. What a special honor! If you have a mother or a father, how might you honor them today?

Notes:

Luke 16:12 And if you have not been trustworthy with someone else's property, who will give you property of your own? (NIV)

Being responsible for things can be incredibly fulfilling. People are counting on you and you deliver. No matter what you are in charge of today, do it to the best of your ability. The reward? You get to be in charge of even better things. What are you responsible for today?

Matthew 12:36 But I tell you that men will have to give account on the day of judgment for every careless word they have spoken. (NIV)

One day you will stand before the creator of the heavens and the earth. You will give an account of your life—including this very day. What do you think of this?

Colossians 3:25 Anyone who does wrong will be repaid for his wrong, and there is no favoritism. (NIV)

Just because you are one of God's favorites does not mean that He will not let you experience the consequences of your behavior. How have the wrongs in your life come back to haunt you?

Galatians 6:7 Do not be deceived: God cannot be mocked. A man reaps what he sows. (NIV)

If you sow seeds of dishonor, you will not be honored. If you sow seeds of arrogance, you will be on the receiving end of arrogance. If you sow critical seeds, you will harvest a critical crop. What seeds of blame have you sown recently? What kind of crop did they yield?

Galatians 6:4 Do your own work well, and then you will have something to be proud of. But don't compare yourself with others. (CEV)

When you take responsibility for your spiritual direction, you grow. When you spend your time comparing your growth with someone else's, you stop growing. Take pride in who God created you to be. How would you describe your growth—spiritually speaking?

Proverbs 6:27 Can a man scoop fire into his lap without his clothes being burned? (NIV)

No! What fire have you been playing with lately?

Proverbs 27:19 As water reflects a face, so a man's heart reflects the man. (NIV)

What is in your heart today? Anger? Fear? Joy? Hope? Peace? Despair? Love? Take a good look. What do you see?

Notes:

Notes:

Acts 20:36 After Paul had finished speaking he knelt down with all of them and prayed. (CEV)

Sometimes very simple acts share your faith more powerfully than you would imagine. Praying with a friend or your family will bring the presence of God into their lives. How is your personal prayer life? How is your family prayer life?

1 Thessalonians 5:17 Pray continually... (NIV)

By reading a verse from this book every day, you are in some way making your whole day a prayer. You are asking God to make the things you do and say a part of His plan for you. How has God shown up in your life?

1 Peter 5:7 Cast all your anxiety on him because he cares for you. (NIV)

You may have noticed how sharing your concerns and worries with someone can help you. This is how it is with God, too. When you talk to Him through prayer, the things that weigh you down get lighter. What are you worrying about today?

Hebrews 4:16 So let us come boldly to the throne of our gracious God. There we will receive his mercy, and we will find grace to help us when we need it most. (NLT)

God is the greatest King the universe has ever known. Yet you can come into His throne room anytime. In fact, He is eager that you do so. Don't hesitate to come before Him today. How do you approach God?

Notes:

Boldly? Flippantly? Eagerly?

Psalm 55:22a Cast your cares on the Lord and he will sustain you. (NIV)

Do you have concerns today? Take a moment to write them down. Write them down, not for God's sake. Write them down for your own sake. What has writing down your prayer concerns done for your prayer life?

Romans 8:26 The Spirit helps us in our weakness. We do not know what we ought to pray for, but the Spirit himself intercedes for us with groans that words cannot express. (NIV)

Sometimes you may not know what to pray for. God will help you. Name the times in your life when you could not even pray.

James 5:16b ... pray for each other so that you may be healed. The earnest prayer of a righteous person has great power and produces wonderful results. (NLV)

Produce wonderful results today. How? Pray for someone. Who can you pray for today?

Notes:

Romans 12:6a In his grace, God has given us different gifts for doing certain things well. (NLT)

"God has given YOU different gifts for doing certain things well." How will you put these things into practice today?

Isaiah 6:8 Then I heard the voice of the Lord saying, "Whom shall I send? And who will go for us?" And I said, "Here am I. Send me!" (NIV)

So you haven't heard the voice of God calling you to do something. Perhaps He is waiting for you to volunteer before He tells you what He wants you to do. What is keeping you from praying this prayer: "Here I am, send me"?

Deuteronomy 30:11-14 Now what I am commanding you today is not too difficult for you or beyond your reach. It is not up in heaven, so that you have to ask, "Who will ascend into heaven to get it and proclaim it to us so we may obey it?" ... No, the word is very near you; it is in your mouth and in your heart so you may obey it. (NIV)

God has been asking something of you lately. You know what it is. Just do it. What do you think God is specifically asking of you at this time?

Acts 1:10,11a They were looking intently up into the sky as he was going, when suddenly two men dressed in white stood beside them. "Men of Galilee," they said, "why do you stand here looking into the sky?" (NIV)

Notes:

This was the first Ascension Day. Jesus' work on earth was finished. But ours has just begun. Why do you sometimes hang back when there are things to be done in the church?

1 Corinthians 9:25 All athletes are disciplined in their training. They do it to win a prize that will fade away, but we do it for an eternal prize. (NLT)

Two things will last: God and the people around you. How can you make Him and them part of the lasting prize that you will go after today?

1 Corinthians 11:1 Follow my example, as I follow the example of Christ. (NIV)

Paul, the author of these words, was confident about his example to others. In what area of your life do you think you could be a good example for others to follow? Are you willing to do it?

Matthew 4:19,20 And he said to them, "Follow me, and I will make you fishers of men." Immediately they left their nets and followed him. (ESV)

Are you willing to follow Jesus? Are you willing to help someone else learn to follow Jesus?

Notes:

Psalm 22:9 Yet you brought me out of the womb; you made me trust in you even at my mother's breast. (NIV)

Faith is really about trust. It's easy to say you believe certain things about God but to trust God with your day, your family, your future, your eternity, well, that's another thing. But God has been teaching you how to trust since you were born. What experience in your life has helped you trust God more?

1 Chronicles 29:11 Thine, O LORD, is the greatness, and the power, and the glory, and the victory, and the majesty: for all that is in the heaven and in the earth is thine; thine is the kingdom, O LORD, and thou art exalted as head above all. (KJV)

Let this verse lift your heart in praise to God. He has the whole world under control—including you. Can you think of a time when God really showed His presence in your life?

Deuteronomy 31:8 The Lord himself goes before you and will be with you; he will never leave you nor forsake you. Do not be afraid; do not be discouraged. (NIV)

Some scary things may be in front of you this week—things you really don't want to do. God is with you. He will always be with you. What in your life reminds you that God will never leave you?

Jeremiah 17:7 But blessed are those who trust in the Lord and have made the Lord their hope and confidence. (NLT)

If you make happiness your goal today, it will elude you. Happiness is a by-product of trusting your day to a God who loves you. Make trusting God your goal today. When in your life were you truly happy?

Romans 8:38,39 I am convinced that neither death nor life, neither angels nor demons, neither the present nor the future, nor any powers, neither height nor depth, nor anything else in all creation, will be able to separate us from the love of God that is in Christ Jesus our Lord. (NIV)

When bad things happen, you may be tempted to let go of God's hand. But know this—God will never let go of yours. When have you felt alone?

Philippians 1:6 And I am certain that God, who began the good work within you, will continue his work until it is finally finished on the day when Christ Jesus returns. (NLT)

Sometimes you may feel like a failure, but God is not finished with you. He's got great plans for you. Looking back at your Christian walk, can you see any progress?

Isaiah 43:2 When you pass through the waters, I [God] will be with you; and when you pass through the rivers, they will not sweep over you. When you walk through the fire, you will not be burned; the flames will not set you ablaze. (NIV)

If you're swamped or on the hot seat today, this verse is for you. What difficult situation are you facing today? Do you trust that God will protect you?

Notes:

Notes:

Leviticus 26:12 I will walk among you and be your God, and you will be my people. (NIV)

Isn't this what you want? A God that walks with you; that cares about what you do and where you go today; a personal God who wants you to be in His family? How are you walking with God every day?

2 Peter 3:18 But grow in the grace and knowledge of our Lord and Savior Jesus Christ. To him be glory both now and forever! Amen. (NIV)

It is all about a growing relationship with Jesus. Letting Him save you. Allowing Him to be Lord of your life. How? Get to know Him (knowledge) and over time experience His love (grace). How would you describe your relationship with Jesus?

Psalm 90:1 Lord, you have been our dwelling place throughout all generations. (NIV)

Your walk with the Lord is not just about you. You are part of a people—a people of God with a history and faith that has been passed down from generation to generation. From one tribe to another, from one language to another. You are not alone. How will knowing you are part of a "people of God" embolden you as you go about living your life today?

2 Corinthians 4:18 So we fix our eyes not on what is seen, but on what is unseen. For what is seen is temporary, but what is unseen is eternal. (NIV)

You see it. You want it. You go after it. But soon, so very soon, it is gone. Sometimes the things that are

Notes:

not seen, like faith, hope, love, God, and eternity, is more important than what is seen. What are your eyes fixed on today?

Jeremiah 9:23,24 This is what the LORD says: "Let not the wise man boast of his wisdom or the strong man boast of his strength or the rich man boast of his riches, but let him who boasts boast about this: that he understands and knows me, that I am the LORD…." (NIV)

You are not somebody because of what you have or what you do. You are somebody because you have a relationship with God. How would you describe your relationship with God?

James 4:8 Come near to God and he will come near to you. (NIV)

Perhaps God seems distant to you lately. Bad things have been happening and you maybe wonder where God is. Could it be that you are the one who is avoiding Him? How much time do you spend talking and listening to God every day?

Dueteronomy 6:6,7 These commandments that I give you today are to be on your hearts. Impress them on your children. Talk about them when you sit at home and when you walk along the road ... (NIV)

What kind of relatioship do you want with God? A close one requires talking (prayer) and listening (reading God's commandments - His Word) multiple times a day. How goes your devotions?

Notes:

***Romans 12:1** Therefore, I urge you, brothers, in view of God's mercy, to offer your bodies as living sacrifices, holy and pleasing to God—this is your spiritual act of worship. (NIV)*

Take this day and all you will do in it—walking, talking, eating, working, playing, praying, laughing, crying—and dedicate it to God. In what way are you sacrificing yourself to God?

***Philippians 3:8** I consider everything a loss compared to the surpassing greatness of knowing Christ Jesus my Lord, for whose sake I have lost all things. (NIV)*

Ask not what God can do for you today; ask what you can do for Him. Ask not what you can gain from God today; ask what you would be willing to lose for Him. What are you willing to do for Him? What are you willing to lose for Him?

***Revelation 4:11** Thou art worthy, O Lord, to receive glory and honor and power: for thou hast created all things, and for thy pleasure they are and were created. (KJV)*

Give God praise today. Just use the words of Revelation 4:11. Repeat them over and over. Why does your giving God praise end up blessing you?

***Philippians 3:10,11** I want to know Christ and ... the fellowship of sharing in his sufferings, becoming like him in his death, and so, somehow, to attain to the resurrection from the dead. (NIV)*

Notes:

There is nothing more important in life than knowing Christ—that's your power source. There is no more important way to know Him than by reading the Bible and talking to Him. How is your relationship with Christ going?

Psalm 24:1 The earth is the Lord's and everything in it, the world, and all who live in it. (NIV)

Everything you plan today, everything you build, everything you produce, everything you acquire, everything you see, touch, or taste... it's all borrowed. In fact, your very life has been loaned to you. How can you use all this that is on loan to you for God's glory?

Luke 9:23 Then [Jesus] said to the crowd, "If any of you wants to be my follower, you must put aside your selfish ambition, shoulder your cross daily, and follow me." (NLT)

A follower of Jesus is a follower of Jesus. You are not a follower of yourself. There is a transfer of control from you to Him. In what areas of your life are you struggling with Jesus for control?

Malachi 1:11 My name will be great among the nations, from the rising to the setting of the sun. (NIV)

God is greater than anything that can be conceived. His greatness covers the universe. And yet as great as God is, His thoughts are of you this day. How does that make you feel?

Notes:

1 John 4:19 We love because he first loved us. (NIV)

Love is the greatest food for an emotionally starving world. But you have to have love before you can give love. God has a huge warehouse full of love. He will give you more than you need so that you can share it with others. How does God's love for you show itself in the lives of those around you?

Song of Songs 8:6,7 The passion of love bursting into flame is more powerful than death, stronger than the grave. Love cannot be drowned by oceans or floods; it cannot be bought, no matter what is offered. (CEV)

Falling in love is probably the most life-altering experience a person can have. And who is behind it? God. Love is His gift to us. Have you ever fallen in love?

Luke 15:20 So he got up and went to his father. But while he was still a long way off, his father saw him and was filled with compassion for him; he ran to his son, threw his arms around him and kissed him. (NIV)

Reconciliation between two people is one of the sweetest uses of God's love. What relationships in your life could use some reconciliation grace?

1 John 3:18 Let us not love with words or tongue but with actions and in truth. (NIV)

Today find one person who needs love. Maybe just talking to or spending time with that person will be exactly what is needed. What can you do today to show someone God's love (and yours)?

1 Peter 4:8 Above all, love each other deeply, because love covers over a multitude of sins. (NIV)

You are not perfect. Your friends are not perfect. Your family is not perfect. And no matter what we do, we end up hurting one another; sometimes unintentionally, sometimes intentionally. But love—the love we give to one another—can help us get along with each other anyway. How has love overcome sin in your relationships?

1 John 3:16 This is how we know what love is: Jesus Christ laid down his life for us. And we ought to lay down our lives for our brothers. (NIV)

Sacrifice. That is what love is. Not loving someone because she or he does something for you. Sacrifice. Have you accepted Jesus' sacrificial love? Are you giving it away?

Ephesians 2:4,5 But because of his great love for us, God, who is rich in mercy, made us alive with Christ even when we were dead in transgressions—it is by grace you have been saved. (NIV)

Are you worth saving? Why would God bother with you? Answer: His love. His great love. His mercy. His rich mercy. Have you received God's love and mercy?

Notes:

Notes:

Proverbs 13:11 Dishonest money dwindles away, but he who gathers money little by little makes it grow. (NIV)

Most of what is good in life happens little by little. A marriage. Personal growth. Parenting. Spiritual growth. So, today, make a little progress. In what areas of your life have you been making a little progress?

Micah 7:8 Do not gloat over me, my enemy! Though I have fallen, I will rise. Though I sit in darkness, the LORD will be my light. (NIV)

You may have fallen. Darkness may be filling your soul. People in your life may be laughing at you behind your back or maybe to your face. But you may just get the last laugh. When has this happened in your life?

Jeremiah 31:25 I will refresh the weary and satisfy the faint. (NIV)

Worn out from the daily grind? Tired from the demands of life? Weary from problems and people? Let God refresh and ultimately satisfy you today. What things in your life have been dragging you down?

1 Peter 5:10 In his kindness God called you to share in his eternal glory by means of Christ Jesus. So after you have suffered a little while, he will restore, support, and strengthen you, and he will place you on a firm foundation. (NLT)

Perhaps you became a Christian recently but you find yourself suffering—and maybe because you are a Christian. Congratulations. You are worthy of the battle. And guess what? You will win in the end. How goes the battle?

James 1:12 Blessed is the one who perseveres under trial because, having stood the test, that person will receive the crown of life that the Lord has promised to those who love him. (NIV)

Life can be good, but often it's just plain hard. Disappointments, failure, discouragement, betrayal, frustration—perhaps you've had your share of these things lately. Keep going. Not in your own strength, but in the strength of the Lord. Your dedication will be rewarded. What hard times have you been dealing with lately?

Isaiah 46:4 Even to your old age and gray hairs I am he, I am he who will sustain you. I have made you and I will carry you; I will sustain you and I will rescue you. (NIV)

When you are weary and feel like giving up, when you can't muster the energy to go forward—He, the one who made you, will carry you. What things are you going through right now that are bringing you down?

Isaiah 43:2,3 "When you go through deep waters and great trouble, I will be with you. When you go through rivers of difficulty, you will not drown! When you walk through the fire of oppression, you will not be burned up. ... For I am the Lord your God." (NLT)

Following God's way does not guarantee you will not have hard times. But the hard times will not defeat you. What rivers and fires have you had to go through?

Notes:

Notes:

Proverbs 18:2 A fool finds no pleasure in understanding but delights in airing his own opinions. (NIV)

When you enter a situation where there is a difference of opinion, try to understand before being understood. Try listening before speaking. If you do, you may just keep or make a friend. Why is it so hard to try to understand someone who doesn't think like you do?

Hebrews 2:18 Since he himself has gone through suffering and testing, he is able to help us when we are being tested. (NLT)

Oh, if only someone truly understood your situation—the pressures, the deadlines, the compromises, the choices, the grief, the anxiety, the stress! There is One who truly understands your situation better than you. He has already been there—Jesus. What do you need to bring to Him in prayer today?

1 Peter 3:8 Finally, all of you, be like-minded, be sympathetic, love one another, be compassionate and humble. (NIV)

So much of life is trying to get along with the people around us—even in the church. The keys are sympathy, love, compassion, and humility. Try these things out on the people in your life and see how it goes. To whom in your life could you try to be a bit more understanding?

Proverbs 18:13 He who answers before listening—that is his folly and his shame. (NIV)

People may ask you a question but they often are not

ready to hear your answer. So when they ask their question, instead of answering right away, ask them what they think. Try it. Can you think of a time when you should've done this?

James 1:19 Understand this, my dear brothers and sisters: You must all be quick to listen, slow to speak, and slow to get angry. (NLT)

Are you angry at someone right now? Maybe something happened a week ago and you are quietly stewing, thinking about how wrong that other person is and what you might like to say if given the chance. Maybe you need to hear the other side before you close the book on this case. Why is it so hard to listen first before speaking your mind?

Psalm 102:1,2 Hear my prayer, O LORD; let my cry for help come to you. Do not hide your face from me when I am in distress. Turn your ear to me; when I call, answer me quickly. (NIV)

Sometimes life hurts so much that all you want to do is cry—but to whom do you cry out? Who will listen? Who will understand? God will and does. In what area of your life do you really, really need an answer from God?

Ecclesiastes 7:3 Sorrow is better than laughter, because a sad face is good for the heart. (NIV)

You can use painful experiences to sense the pain of others and lift them up. What experiences can you use to understand a friend's sorrow?

Notes:

Notes:

Psalm 53:2 God looks down from heaven on the sons of men to see if there are any who understand, any who seek God. (NIV)

We are born seekers. Looking for friends. Looking for happiness. Looking for purpose and meaning. Looking for security. Looking for peace. It's really all a search for God, isn't it? How is your search going?

Acts 26:19 "So then, King Agrippa, I was not disobedient to the vision from heaven." (NIV)

God gave Paul a vision—a bold vision of sharing His love with those that did not know it. Despite hardships and setbacks, Paul followed it. What vision has God given to you and how well are you following through with it?

Psalm 71:18 Even when I am old and gray, do not forsake me, O God, till I declare your power to the next generation your might to all who are to come. (NIV)

To experience the wonder and power of God for a lifetime and to pass it on to others—this is the essence of a life well lived. Did you have grandparents that passed on the faith? How did they do this?

Proverbs 27:7 A person who is full refuses honey, but even bitter food tastes sweet to the hungry. (NLT)

Hunger is good. Pain is good. Want is good. Need is good. If we were not aware of any need, what would drive us to each other? What would drive us to God?

Notes:

Mark 13:32,33 No one knows about that day or hour, not even the angels in heaven, nor the Son, but only the Father. Be on guard! Be alert! You do not know when that time will come. (NIV)

If you knew Jesus was coming and the world was ending in one month, what things would you want to do? What if you knew Jesus was coming in a year? Ten years? Why would it make any difference when He is coming again?

Jeremiah 32:39 And I will give them one heart and one purpose: to worship me forever, for their own good and for the good of all their descendants. (NIV)

Can you imagine a group of people that would actually have this one heart and purpose? No wonder it would get passed down to the next generation. What does this verse reveal about God?

Romans 8:28 And we know that in all things God works for the good of those who love him, who have been called according to his purpose. (NIV)

What you might consider "good things" will happen in your life. Bad things, too. But all of it can be used by God for His purpose. How is this verse helping you these days? Where in your life are you struggling to apply this verse?

Notes:

1 Peter 2:17 Show proper respect to everyone.... (NIV)

If you respect others, they will respect you. Whom can you show respect to today? How are you going to do it?

Luke 12:3 What you have said in the dark will be heard in the daylight, and what you have whispered in the ear in the inner rooms will be proclaimed from the roofs. (NIV)

Talking about people behind their backs is very tempting, and talking about them with a bunch of friends makes you feel like you are part of the group. And what is the harm? The person being talked about will never know, right? Really? Read this verse again. Perhaps read it a few times. Why do we gossip?

Psalm 69:6 May those who hope in you not be disgraced because of me, O Lord, the Lord Almighty; may those who seek you not be put to shame because of me, O God. (NIV)

When you go about your business today, you not only represent yourself and your family, but you also represent the God who created this universe. Walk proud. Make God proud. What impression do you give others about God?

Matthew 5:23,24 Therefore, if you are offering your gift at the altar and there remember that your brother has something against you, leave your gift there in front of the altar. First go and be reconciled to your brother; then come and offer your gift. (NIV)

Someone thinks you said or did this or that and they are offended. They should come to you directly with their offense. Instead, they go to others. Maybe you need to go to them. With whom do you need to clear the air?

Notes:

Proverbs 18:8 The words of a gossip are like choice morsels; they go down to a man's inmost parts. (NIV)

Too much food will put on extra weight. When you gossip, it's like feeding your soul high-fat junk food. Why do you gossip? What does it do for you? Who gets hurt? With what spiritual "health food" can you replace gossip?

Matthew 18:15 "If your brother sins against you, go and show him his fault, just between the two of you. If he listens to you, you have won your brother over." (NIV)

So many problems in school, at home, and in the church would be avoided if we followed Matthew 18:15. If you need to, call up someone who wronged you and win him or her over. Why do you talk about people behind their backs?

James 4:11 My friends, don't say cruel things about others! If you do, or if you condemn others, you are condemning God's Law. And if you condemn the Law, you put yourself above the Law. (CEV)

It sometimes feels good to say cruel things about others—especially when you are with a group of people who agree with you—especially if the person you are talking about is not there to defend themselves. It feels good in the short run. Why doesn't it feel good in the long run?

Notes:

Galatians 6:9 ***So let's not get tired of doing what is good. At just the right time we will reap a harvest of blessing if we don't give up. (NLT)***

The promise of reward gets many to start a course. The actual reward is only given to those who finish it. Keep doing what is good. You'll get there. What in your life needs finishing?

Matthew 6:19,20 ***"Do not store up for yourselves treasures on earth, where moth and rust destroy, and where thieves break in and steal. But store up for yourselves treasures in heaven, where moth and rust do not destroy … ." (NIV)***

People say "you can't take it with you!" but they are wrong. What you do for others stores up treasures in heaven. Where are you storing your treasure these days?

Ecclesiastes 5:19 ***It is a good thing to receive wealth from God and the good health to enjoy it. To enjoy your work and accept your lot in life—that is indeed a gift from God. (NLT)***

Feeling good about your wealth and possessions comes when you do good things with your wealth and possessions. What good are you doing with your wealth and possessions?

Psalm 23:6 ***Surely goodness and love will follow me all the days of my life, and I will dwell in the house of the Lord forever. (NIV)***

God blesses you daily with His love and goodness. He also promises you the best gift ever—heaven. When have you experienced God's goodness?

***2 Thessalonians 2:16,17** May our Lord Jesus Christ himself and God our Father, who loved us and by his grace gave us eternal encouragement and good hope, encourage your hearts and strengthen you in every good deed and word. (NIV)*

As you go out into the world today in the hope of saying and doing good things, take with you the encouragement of God. What has the encouragement of God done for you?

***Acts 20:24** However, I consider my life worth nothing to me, if only I may finish the race and complete the task the Lord Jesus has given me—the task of testifying to the gospel of God's grace. (NIV)*

You have a God-given task today—to share the goodness of God with those in your life. What good has God been in your life? Are you sharing it with others?

***Psalm 23:6** Surely goodness and love will follow me all the days of my life, and I will dwell in the house of the LORD forever. (NIV)*

Look back on your life. How has goodness and love followed you so far? What do you think it will be like in heaven?

Notes:

Notes:

1 Timothy 6:7-9 For we brought nothing into the world, and we can take nothing out of it. But if we have food and clothing, we will be content with that. Those who want to get rich fall into temptation and a trap and into many foolish and harmful desires that plunge people into ruin and destruction. (NIV)

Contentment or entrapment. Which is it going to be today?

Galatians 2:6 God does not judge by external appearances. (NIV)

Phew... isn't that a relief? Perfect hair isn't necessary. Neither are pearly white teeth, a flawless figure, big muscles, the latest clothes, or clear skin. God loves you. No amount of dieting, primping, shopping, or styling can make Him love you more than He does. Do you judge others by outward appearance? How about yourself?

1 Timothy 6:6 Yet true godliness with contentment is itself great wealth. (NLT)

Not as tall as you want to be? Not as attractive as you would like? Not as successful as some? But are you living a God-honoring life? You have all you need and, by the way, more than most. How wealthy are you?

Ecclesiastes 3:13 That everyone may eat and drink, and find satisfaction in all his toil—this is the gift of God. (NIV)

School. Work. Chores. A joy? Yes, if you have the right understanding of them. First, there is the joy of a job well done. Second, there is the fruit of doing a good job. What fruit do you think can come from your toil?

Haggai 1:6 You have planted much, but have harvested little. You eat, but never have enough. You drink, but never have your fill. You put on clothes, but are not warm. You earn wages, only to put them in a purse with holes in it. (NIV)

You want the latest things. You pursue them and acquire them. But are you satisfied? There's always more to want, pursue, acquire. Why aren't we content with what we already have?

Philippians 4:12 I know what it is to be in need, and I know what it is to have plenty. I have learned the secret of being content in any and every situation, whether well fed or hungry, whether living in plenty or in want. (NIV)

There is a secret to being content in all situations. It is found in Philippians 4:13. Find it. Read it. Live it. What is the secret of being content?

Hebrews 13:5 Keep your lives free from the love of money and be content with what you have, because God has said, "Never will I leave you; never will I forsake you." (NIV)

Use money; love God. Money comes and goes. God will be with you forever. Are you in charge of your money or is money in charge of you?

Notes:

Notes:

***James 4:13,14a* Look here, you who say, "Today or tomorrow we are going to a certain town and will stay there a year. We will do business there and make a profit." How do you know what your life will be like tomorrow? (NLT)**

There is a phrase you can add to all your dreams about tomorrow that sort of puts things into perspective. Just add, "the Lord willing." "I will do this or that, the Lord willing." Have you heard someone use this phrase before? Does it make sense to you?

***Psalm 88:13* But I cry to you for help, O LORD; in the morning my prayer comes before you. (NIV)**

Do you need help today? Do you want help today? Ask for it. Do it now. In what area of your life do you need help?

***John 8:7* When they kept on questioning him, he straightened up and said to them, "If any one of you is without sin, let him be the first to throw a stone at her." (NIV)**

It is so easy to see the sin in others. Look at yourself before you condemn someone else. "People who live in glass houses shouldn't throw stones." Who have you condemned lately?

***Philippians 2:3* Don't be selfish; don't try to impress others. Be humble, thinking of others as better than yourselves. (NLT)**

Do I fit in with this group or with that? Do I fit in at all with any group? Do people like me? What do they think of me? Me, me, me. Who can you be a friend to today? What do you have to offer?

Psalm 23:1-3 The LORD is my shepherd, I shall not be in want. He makes me lie down in green pastures, he leads me beside quiet waters, he restores my soul. He guides me in paths of righteousness for his name's sake. (NIV)

Running and controlling your life is exhausting. Remember you are one of the sheep, not the shepherd. What area of your life do you need to give to the Lord today?

Obadiah 1:3,4 "The pride of your heart has deceived you, you who live in the clefts of the rocks and make your home on the heights, you who say to yourself, 'Who can bring me down to the ground?' Though you soar like the eagle and make your nest among the stars, from there I will bring you down," declares the LORD. (NIV)

Pride goes before a fall. When did your pride bring you down?

Proverbs 27:2 Let someone else praise you, not your own mouth—a stranger, not your own lips. (NLT)

No one has said good things about you lately. You wonder if anyone notices you. Be patient. Someone will notice you. God already has. Why do we as human beings need praise and recognition? Why do you?

Notes:

Notes:

Acts 2:46,47 Every day they continued to meet together. ... They broke bread in their homes and ate together with glad and sincere hearts, praising God and enjoying the favor of all the people. And the Lord added to their number daily those who were being saved. (NIV)

The most important church is the one that meets in your home—your family. How is the church in your own home going? Have you shared your walk with your family? Why? Why not?

Hebrews 10:25 Let us not give up meeting together, as some are in the habit of doing, but let us encourage one another ... (NIV)

You cannot make it alone. All humans meet in groups of like-minded people to be challenged and encouraged in their common beliefs. If you want to walk with God, you must get together with others who want the same thing. Do you have a group to challenge and encourage your walk of faith?

Romans 12:4,5 Just as our bodies have many parts and each part has a special function, so it is with Christ's body. (NLT)

We are many parts of one body, and we all belong to each other. Look around at the people in your life. They are different from you. You are different from them. That is the way it's supposed to be. Where have you experienced a sense of unity?

Romans 15:5 May the God who gives endurance and encouragement give you a spirit of unity among

yourselves as you follow Christ Jesus... (NIV)

You need to be a part of a group that is united and following Christ. With this combination in your life, you will get the encouragement you need to persevere when things get tough. Are you part of a group like that?

Proverbs 15:17 Better a meal of vegetables where there is love than a fattened calf with hatred. (NIV)

The good life is less about getting and enjoying good things, and more about getting and enjoying good people. How has this been reflected in how you spend your time lately?

1 Corinthians 12:27 Now you are the body of Christ, and each one of you is a part of it. (NIV)

Paul, the author of these words, is talking about the church. He says that each person is a part of it and that all the parts together become Christ's body, which is the church. How are you a part of the church?

Acts 21:5 But when our time was up, we left and continued on our way. All the disciples and their wives and children accompanied us out of the city, and there on the beach we knelt to pray. (NIV)

Spiritual values are powerfully taught in the context of your family. Try this: Take this book to the kitchen table. Find out what your family's prayer needs are. What does your family do in terms of Bible reading and prayer?

Notes:

Notes:

***Philemon 6** I pray that you may be active in sharing your faith, so that you will have a full understanding of every good thing we have in Christ. (NIV)*

You don't know what you have until you share it with someone else. How does sharing your faith with others benefit you?

***1 Peter 3:15** You must worship Christ as Lord of your life. And if you are asked about your Christian hope, always be ready to explain it. (NLT)*

Look for opportunities to share your walk with God. Just share what you are doing every day to stay close to God. How would you explain your hope if someone asked you about it today?

***1 Kings 18:37** "Answer me, O LORD, answer me, so these people will know that you, O LORD, are God, and that you are turning their hearts back again." (NIV)*

Have you ever prayed this prayer—that God would show himself to your friends, to skeptical people you know, or maybe to yourself?

***2 Corinthians 9:8** And God will generously provide all you need. Then you will always have everything you need and plenty left over to share with others. (NLT)*

Ever wonder why God has blessed you with so much? It is because He has people in mind that need your help. Who in your world needs your help?

Notes:

Colossians 4:5 Live wisely among those who are not believers, and make the most of every opportunity. (NLT)

What you do today and how you do it will make an impression on someone—positively or negatively. That means what you do today and how you do it is important. That means you are important. What opportunities have you had lately to communicate your faith?

Ecclesiastes 11:4 Whoever watches the wind will not plant; whoever looks at the clouds will not reap. (NIV)

You may have to live with the regret of what-might-have-been if you wait for the "perfect moment" to share your faith with someone. What holds you back from sowing seeds?

Romans 1:8 First, I thank my God through Jesus Christ for all of you, because your faith is being reported all over the world. (NIV)

Can you imagine someone thanking God for you because your faith—your story—is being shared with people all over the world? It could happen. God uses ordinary people like you to spread His love. How has God used your faith story to reach others?

Notes:

Proverbs 30:15 The leech has two daughters. "Give! Give!" they cry. (NIV)

We live in a "someone should do it for me" culture where we have rights to health, wealth, and happiness. Instead of waiting for or demanding a handout, why not put some of your own effort into the task at hand? Where in your life do you need to be more industrious?

Proverbs 10:4 Lazy people are soon poor; hard workers get rich. (NLT)

Today is a new opportunity to make things happen. What kind of worker are you? What is the purpose of work?

1 Corinthians 9:26 So I run with purpose in every step. I am not just shadowboxing. (NLT)

Today make a goal to do something that will bring a smile to God's face. Write it down on your "to do" list—and then do something about it. What are some of your goals for your family? For work? For school? For fun? For God?

Ecclesiastes 11:6 Sow your seed in the morning, and at evening let not your hands be idle, for you do not know which will succeed, whether this or that, or whether both will do equally well. (NIV)

It is hard to tell what a plant will one day look like from the seed. You have to plant it and wait for it to grow. In your life you will sow many seeds; you will try many things. Some seeds will grow and some won't.

Some things you try will work out and some will not. What seeds can you see growing in your life?

Proverbs 14:23 All hard work brings a profit, but mere talk leads only to poverty. (NIV)

Just do it! Are you a talker or a worker?

Ecclesiastes 2:24,25 A man can do nothing better than to eat and drink and find satisfaction in his work. This too, I see, is from the hand of God, for without him, who can eat or find enjoyment? (NIV)

God created the universe in six days with His mighty hand, and when He looked at what He had created He said, "It is very good." You have the opportunity to create things with your own hands, too. Enjoy! What do you enjoy creating?

Ephesians 4:16 From him the whole body, joined and held together by every supporting ligament, grows and builds itself up in love, as each part does its work. (NIV)

Many who say they want to grow spiritually somehow think great things will happen while they sit on the bench watching others do the work. The Christian life is a team sport. Be a player, not a spectator. Are you a player or a spectator?

Notes:

Notes:

Acts 4:12 ***Salvation is found in no one else, for there is no other name under heaven given to men by which we must be saved. (NIV)***

The world wants you to believe that many roads lead to life, salvation, fulfillment, or heaven, but God says there is only one. Every other person, religion, belief system, or lifestyle will fail you. Jesus is the only one who won't fail you. What are you counting on for your salvation?

John 20:31 ***But these [words of the Bible] are written that you may believe that Jesus is the Christ, the Son of God, and that by believing you may have life in his name. (NIV)***

If you want life in the name of Jesus, then you must get to know Him—that is what reading a little bit of the Bible every day is all about. Keep it up! How would you describe your relationship with Jesus?

Psalm 143:8 ***Let the morning bring me word of your unfailing love, for I have put my trust in you. Show me the way I should go, for to you I lift up my soul. (NIV)***

"Give me a word today, Lord. A word that says You care for me, a word that reassures me that my trust in You is not in vain. Then show me what I should do." Are you ready to give yourself to God today?

Revelation 3:20 ***Here I am! I stand at the door and knock. If anyone hears my voice and opens the door, I will come in and eat with him, and he with me. (NIV)***

Notes:

Jesus, the one through whom the world was created, wants to sit down with you—face to face, friend to friend—and eat with you. He's just waiting for an invite. How has God knocked on your door lately?

Mark 10:17 As Jesus started on his way, a man ran up to him and fell on his knees before him. "Good teacher," he asked, "what must I do to inherit eternal life?" (NIV)

A good question but the wrong one. There is nothing you can do to inherit eternal life. Jesus did it for you. You just need to accept it. That is the one thing you could do. Oh, and God is willing to help you do that as well! Have you accepted God's gift of eternal life through what Jesus did for you on the cross?

Psalm 86:11 Teach me your way, O Lord, and I will walk in your truth; give me an undivided heart, that I may fear your name. (NIV)

There are basically two ways to play the game of life. One is to live as if there is a God. The other is to live as if there isn't. Today you may be tempted to cover both bases. Make a choice. Do you have an undivided heart?

Proverbs 16:3 Commit to the LORD whatever you do, and he will establish your plans. (NIV)

You want success with school, friends, family, sports, life—start with your commitment to the Lord. What can you commit to the Lord today?

Notes:

***Ephesians 4:32* Be kind and compassionate to one another, forgiving each other, just as in Christ God forgave you. (NIV)**

Need some motivation to be compassionate toward someone who has hurt you? Look at how much God loves you and is compassionate toward you. Who do you need to show compassion to today?

***1 John 3:17* If someone has enough money to live well and sees a brother or sister in need but shows no compassion—how can God's love be in that person? (NLT)**

Talk is cheap. How about some action today? What can you do to share the love of God in some practical way?

***James 2:15,16* Suppose a brother or sister is without clothes and daily food. If one of you says to him, "Go, I wish you well; keep warm and well fed," but does nothing about his physical needs, what good is it? (NIV)**

The dictionary says that compassion is only compassion when you actually do something to help solve the problem. What problem are you going to help solve today?

***Lamentations 3:21,22* Yet this I call to mind and therefore I have hope: Because of the Lord's great love we are not consumed, for his compassions never fail. (NIV)**

Today is a good day to be alive. You may not have it all together. You may not even know how to put it together. It is still a good day. The Lord can put it together. What in your life do you need God to put together?

Leviticus 19:9,10 When you reap the harvest of your land do not reap to the very edges of your field or gather the gleanings of your harvest. Do not go over your vineyard a second time or pick up the grapes that have fallen. Leave them for the poor and the alien. I am the LORD your God. (NIV)

Helping someone help themselves not only makes that person feel good, but it also makes you feel good, too. How can you help someone today in such a way that you'll feel that you've been helped too?

Ephesians 4:32 Be kind and compassionate to one another, forgiving each other, just as in Christ God forgave you. (NIV)

What if you don't feel kind and compassionate today? It is hard to forgive someone who just lied to you, mistreated you, or took something from you. It is hard, but try this: think about how poorly you have treated God lately, and then realize He has forgiven you. How does knowing God has forgiven you help you to forgive others?

Notes:

Notes:

1 Corinthians 9:25 All athletes are disciplined in their training. They do it to win a prize that will fade away, but we do it for an eternal prize. (NLT)

Whatever work or games you are involved in today, make sure you do your best for God. What are you striving for? Is God a part of it?

Proverbs 25:16 If you find honey, eat just enough—too much of it, and you will vomit. (NIV)

Sometimes less is more. Perhaps the good things of life taste better when they come around less often. Today, what can you do without? What can you do with less of?

1 Corinthians 9:27 I discipline my body like an athlete, training it to do what it should. Otherwise, I fear that after preaching to others I myself might be disqualified. (NLT)

If you are an athlete, you know that growth in a sport depends on your willingness to work at it. Spiritual growth is like that, too. What is your spiritual training program?

Proverbs 6:6-8 Go to the ant, you sluggard; consider its ways and be wise! It has no commander, no overseer or ruler, yet it stores its provisions in summer and gathers its food at harvest. (NIV)

Self-discipline is the ability to voluntarily forgo one's gratification in the present so as to maximize it in the future. What do you want in the future that will require a sacrifice in the present?

Notes:

Proverbs 20:13 Do not love sleep or you will grow poor; stay awake and you will have food to spare. (NIV)

You are out of bed. The new day is before you. Go at it! Do you have a hard time getting up in the morning? Why or why not?

1 Corinthians 6:20 God bought you with a high price. So you must honor God with your body. (NLT)

You are not your own. Your body has been given to you on loan. God gave it to you so that you could serve Him with passion and energy. How are you treating this gift?

Psalm 1:2 But they delight in the law of the LORD, meditating on it day and night. (NLT)

Every morning, read the Bible and pray with someone. You learn about each other and what is on your hearts when you talk to God together. Do you have a consistent time of talking and listening to God with family?

Notes:

***Jude 1:24,25** To Him who is able to keep you from falling and to present you before his glorious presence without fault and with great joy—to the only God our Savior be glory, majesty, power and authority, through Jesus Christ our Lord, before all ages, now and forevermore! Amen. (NIV)*

The great prize—the great reward that will be presented to the great King of all the earth—is it not you? Do you get a sense of how important you are to God?

***Isaiah 64:8** Yet, O LORD, you are our Father. We are the clay, you are the potter; we are all the work of your hand. (NIV)*

When you woke up this morning and looked in the mirror you probably didn't realize that you are a priceless, incredible creation of the greatest artist that there ever was. How might knowing that you are the direct work of God's hand influence how you do things today?

***1 John 3:1** How great is the love the Father has lavished on us, that we should be called children of God! And that is what we are! (NIV)*

Have you ever day-dreamed of being the son or daughter of royalty? Like maybe there was a mix up at the hospital but now the truth has come out: You are a prince. You are a princess. Guess what? It is not a dream. What does it mean that you are a child of God?

***Ephesians 4:7** However, he has given each one of us a special gift through the generosity of Christ. (NLT)*

That's right. You are gifted. Oh, there's a good chance you don't see yourself in that light. But just step into God's light today—because gifted is how He sees you. What special abilities has Christ given you?

Notes:

Ephesians 2:10 For we are God's workmanship, created in Christ Jesus to do good works, which God prepared in advance for us to do. (NIV)

There is no handiwork that can equal God's workmanship: you! He has created you with special gifts and talents to use for His glory. How are you using your unique abilities for God's work?

Jeremiah 1:5 Before I formed you in the womb I knew you, before you were born I set you apart. (NIV)

With so many people in the world, you may not feel important or special. You are! God worked very carefully to make you the unique, precious person you are. When was the last time you felt special?

Psalm 8:5 Yet you made [humans] only a little lower than God and crowned them with glory and honor. (NLT)

You may be wondering if anything you plan today will make a difference in the big picture—after all, you are but a speck of dust on the earth. But in God's eyes you are the crown of a vast universe. Is it easier to see yourself as a crown of glory or as a speck of dust?

Notes:

Psalm 27:14 *Wait on the LORD: be of good courage, and he shall strengthen thine heart: wait, I say, on the LORD. (KJV)*

It takes real courage to be patient when things don't go as planned. But God's plan is not always your plan. His is better. Wait for it. What are you waiting on the Lord for right now?

Job 17:11 *My days have passed, my plans are shattered, and so are the desires of my heart. (NIV)*

Plans give you energy and keep you going forward. When plans get shattered, so does your heart. The Lord can renew your plans or give you new plans. And when that happens, your heart will be restored. Wait and see. What plans of yours have been shattered lately?

Psalm 62:1 *My soul waits in silence for God only; From Him is my salvation. (NASB)*

Sometimes this is all you can do. You are frustrated. You tried all you can think of to make the situation better. But nothing works. Leave the problem. Sit in silence. Call on the Lord. Then wait. Why is this often our last resort?

Psalm 40:1 *I waited patiently for the Lord; he turned to me and heard my cry. (NIV)*

You have felt the hurt of being alone. You wanted the hurt to go away, but the emptiness inside remained. You wanted to cry. Maybe you did. God heard your cry. Bring your hurts to God in prayer today. What hurts are you dealing with lately?

Notes:

Ephesians 4:2 Be humble and gentle. Be patient with each other, making allowance for each other's faults because of your love. (NLT)

Your friends are not perfect. Your co-workers are not perfect. Your kids are not perfect. Your spouse is not perfect. You are not perfect either. So lighten up! Whose faults bother you more—yours or others? Why?

Lamentations 3:44 You have covered yourself with a cloud so that no prayer can get through. (NIV)

You pray to God, but lately it seems like you are just talking to yourself. "Are you there, God?" you ask. He is. Keep praying. He hears you. Just wait. Why is it hard to wait?

2 Thessalonians 1:6 God is just: He will pay back trouble to those who trouble you. (NIV)

There are people in your life—people who have mistreated you, passed you by, talked negatively behind your back or maybe even to your face. And they are getting away with it. You are suffering; they are doing well. You want so badly for them to pay for their trouble-making. They will. Who is giving you trouble these days?

Notes:

Acts 8:30,31 Then Philip ran up to the chariot and heard the man reading Isaiah the prophet. "Do you understand what you are reading?" Philip asked. "How can I," he said, "unless someone explains it to me?" So he invited Philip to come up and sit with him. (NIV)

Philip helped the man in the chariot understand what he was reading in the Bible. Most people need help reading the Bible. God perhaps set it up that way. Who has helped you in the past? Who can you help?

Luke 6:40 The student is not above the teacher, but everyone who is fully trained will be like their teacher. (NIV)

If you want to make a disciple you must first be a disciple. Being a disciple requires training. So who is training you? Oh, and the goal of the training - to be like Jesus. Who are you training to be like Jesus?

Matthew 28: 18-20 Then Jesus came to them and said, "All authority in heaven and on earth has been given to me. Therefore go and make disciples of all nations, baptizing them ... and teaching them to obey everything I have commanded you. And surely I am with you always, to the very end of the age. (NIV)

Jesus made only 12 disciples in His time on earth. They changed the world. Who are you discipling?

Titus 2:7 In everything set them an example by doing what is good. (NIV)

Notes:

If you are a follower of Christ then you are a teacher. There are people in your life that look to you for how they should be. Who are you teaching? What are you teaching them?

Psalm 19:14 May the words of my mouth and the meditation of my heart be pleasing in your sight, O LORD, my Rock and my Redeemer. (NIV)

The words you use today—words that bring hope or words that bring hurt; the thoughts you think—thoughts of good or thoughts of evil; these define who you are today. What can you think about and what can you say that will be pleasing to the Lord today?

Colossians 4:5 Live wisely among those who are not believers, and make the most of every opportunity. (NLT)

You have the potential of influencing every person you meet. Don't waste opportunities. Be wise. Let others know how you are growing in your walk with God. How is your walk with God? Do you share your walk with others?

2 Corinthians 3:3 You show that you are a letter from Christ, the result of our ministry, written not with ink but with the Spirit of the living God, not on tablets of stone but on tablets of human hearts. (NIV)

Your life is a letter. What kind of a letter are you? How do the people in your life read of God when they read you? How are you letting Christ write your life?

Notes:

Psalm 119:32 I run in the path of your commands, for you have set my heart free. (NIV)

Run free today. Don't walk, run. Run free in your business. Run free in your household. Run free in your daily life. Run with total reckless abandonment following the path laid out by God Himself. Why does following God's commands lead to freedom?

Romans 6:22 But now that you have been set free from sin and have become slaves to God, the benefit you reap leads to holiness, and the result is eternal life. (NIV)

Everyone is a slave to someone or something. What or whom would you like to be freed from?

Psalm 25:17 The troubles of my heart have multiplied; free me from my anguish. (NIV)

One thing goes wrong—then another. Oh, to be free of these troubles! What troubles are taking a toll on you these days?

2 Peter 2:19 They promise freedom, but they themselves are slaves of sin and corruption. For you are a slave to whatever controls you. (NLT)

Is it money? Is it food? Is it your "to do" list? Is it your need to be liked? Is it your desire to be the center of attention? Is it your fear? Is it your insecurity? Is it the internet? Is it your hobby? Is it your doubt? What controls you? What takes your time? What takes your energy? Whatever it is, you have become its slave. What things seek to control your life?

Notes:

Proverbs 12:25 An anxious heart weighs a man down but a kind word cheers him up. (NIV)

Worry can be a huge weight. It drags you down. It's like running with an iron ball attached to your legs. Then come some kind words. Off falls the weight. You feel free. Go out today and free some people with your kind words. What are some kind things you could say to the people in your life?

Isaiah 44:22 I have swept away your sins like a cloud. I have scattered your offenses like the morning mist. Oh, return to me, for I have paid the price to set you free. (NLT)

You may have said or done things that left you ashamed or guilty. One joy of being a Christian is living for the future instead of in the past. God has invited everyone—even those with bad track records—to turn to Him and be saved. What burdens are you carrying?

2 Corinthians 3:17 Now the Lord is the Spirit, and where the Spirit of the Lord is, there is freedom. (NIV)

Ultimate freedom is about relationships—those to whom you are connected. Who are you connected to? How would a connection to the Spirit of God give you freedom?

Notes:

Psalm 8:1 O LORD, our Lord, how majestic is your name in all the earth! You have set your glory above the heavens. (NIV)

Take a moment tonight. Step outside. Look up at the night sky. Let your mind drift out to the moon, the distant planets, and the far-flung stars. God is beyond all of it. When was the last time you were overwhelmed by God?

Psalm 19:1 The heavens declare the glory of God; and the firmament sheweth his handywork. (KJV)

As you go through your day, see God in the world around you. See His power. See His creativity. See His beauty. See His attention to detail. See His use of variety. Then realize you are His best creation. How have you seen God in nature? What does creation tell you about God?

1 Chronicles 16:23 Sing to the LORD, all the earth; proclaim his salvation day after day. (NIV)

Can you hear the singing? Can you hear the praise of the whole earth—in the voices of God's people, in the whisper of the wind, in the rustle of the leaves, in the melody of the birds, in the cackles, the snorts, the calls, the barks? Listen. What did you hear?

Romans 1:20 For ever since the world was created, people have seen the earth and sky. Through everything God made, they can clearly see his invisible qualities—his eternal power and divine nature. So they have no excuse for not knowing God. (NLT)

When in your life were you overwhelmed with a sense of God's presence in creation?

Ephesians 5:19 Speak to one another with psalms, hymns and spiritual songs. Sing and make music in your heart to the Lord. (NIV)

Music is a language that slips past well-guarded hearts and souls. It connects us to God and people in mysterious and wondrous ways. How has music helped connect you with God? With others?

Psalm 8:3,4 When I consider your heavens, the work of your fingers, the moon and the stars, which you have set in place, what is man that you are mindful of him, the son of man that you care for him? (NIV)

The starry night has inspired human beings to contemplate their place in the universe since Abraham was directed by God to do so. Perhaps you have done this too. What did you figure out?

Genesis 2:3 God blessed the seventh day and made it holy, because on it he rested from all the work of creating that he had done. (NIV)

If God took one day in seven to break from work and just reflect on what He had done the previous six days, maybe you should too. How can you make that happen this Sunday?

Notes:

Notes:

Psalm 5:3 In the morning, O Lord, you hear my voice; in the morning I lay my requests before you and wait in expectation. (NIV)

What a great way to start the day! What are you waiting for or expecting from God?

Proverbs 16:3 Commit to the Lord whatever you do, and your plans will succeed. (NIV)

It is easy to get caught up in one's own plans and activities and all that it takes to succeed in those plans and activities. Without God all these plans and activities are bound to fail. What are you doing today? Have you prayed about it?

Isaiah 49:23 "Those who hope in me will not be disappointed." (NIV)

Great expectations. You get married with great expectations. You begin a job with great expectations. You start a new friendship with great expectations. Then come the great disappointments. But things are different with God. How have you been disappointed in your life? What got you through?

1 Peter 1:3 All praise to God, the Father of our Lord Jesus Christ. It is by his great mercy that we have been born again, because God raised Jesus Christ from the dead. Now we live with great expectation. (NLT)

When things don't turn out as anticipated, expectations often lead to disappointments. How does knowing Jesus turn disappointments into great expectations?

Notes:

James 5:8 You too, be patient and stand firm, because the Lord's coming is near. (NIV)

Someday—soon, we hope—Jesus will show up in great power and glory. It will be worth waiting for! How does knowing about the day of the Lord's coming affect your everyday life?

Ephesians 1:18,19 I pray that your hearts will be flooded with light so that you can understand the wonderful future he has promised to those he called. (NLT)

An old man, worn and weather-beaten, sitting in a musty jail cell in the Middle East 2,000 years ago, wrote these words in a letter to people just like you. His prayer changed their lives. It can change yours, too. How has God's Word changed you?

John 12:13 They took palm branches and went out to meet him, shouting, "Hosanna!" "Blessed is he who comes in the name of the Lord!" "Blessed is the King of Israel!" (NIV)

On Palm Sunday, 2,000 years ago, the people in Jerusalem had high, but misguided expectations for the long-awaited Messiah—Jesus. Some 2,000 years later, what expectations do you have for Jesus?

Notes:

Joshua 1:8 Do not let this Book of the Law depart from your mouth; meditate on it day and night, so that you may be careful to do everything written in it. Then you will be prosperous and successful. (NIV)

The words "prosperous" and "successful" do not usually go with "meditate" do they? But thinking good thoughts over and over (meditation) can certainly keep us focused on how we ought to live. And who knows more about how we ought to live than the one who created us? Where in God's Word are you currently meditating?

Matthew 4:4 "People need more than bread for their life; they must feed on every word of God." (NLT)

The Bible is God's way of communicating with you in a tangible way. Do you read the Bible at lunch or dinner time? If you have children, are you sharing the Bible stories with them on a daily basis? How are you accessing the Word of God in a daily way?

2 Peter 1:21 For prophecy never had its origin in the will of man, but men spoke from God as they were carried along by the Holy Spirit. (NIV)

The Bible was written by more than 40 authors over thousands of years and yet has one single message. Why? The Holy Spirit inspired the words. The same Holy Spirit promises to inspire you as you read them. When have you felt God was speaking to you from the Bible?

Deuteronomy 11:18 Fix these words of mine in your hearts and minds; tie them as symbols on your

Notes:

hands and bind them on your foreheads. (NIV)

The Word of God cannot get to your mind and from your mind to your heart unless it is first in your hands and in front of your eyes. How is this book helping you get God's Word into your everyday life?

2 Timothy 2:9 God's word is not chained. (NIV)

Paul wrote these words from prison—while in chains. You may be imprisoned by whatever is holding you back in life, but the Word of God can eventually set you free. How are you going to get the Word of God in your life today?

1 Peter 1:24,25 As the Scriptures say, "People are like grass; their beauty is like a flower in the field. The grass withers and the flower fades. But the word of the Lord remains forever." And that word is the Good News that was preached to you. (NLT)

Your body, strong though it may be, is like a flower that will fall to the ground. But as you take the Word of God into your life, you have something in you that will stand forever. How do you think the Word of God in you will last forever?

Acts 2:41 Those who accepted [Peter's] message were baptized, and about three thousand were added to their number that day. (NIV)

This is what happened at the first Pentecost when the Word of God was spoken to people. Who in your life needs to hear the Word of God?

Notes:

1 Peter 1:7 These [trials] have come so that your faith—of greater worth than gold, which perishes even though refined by fire—may be proved genuine and may result in praise, glory and honor when Jesus Christ is revealed. (NIV)

Testing helps you know who you really are—your strengths and weaknesses. And it proves to you and God that your faith is real. How has your faith been tested? How did you come out in the test?

Luke 16:11 So if you have not been trustworthy in handling worldly wealth, who will trust you with true riches? (NIV)

Do you want more money? More influence? More opportunities? Do you want more friends? Do you want more responsibilities? Do you want more? Maybe God is waiting to see what you do with what you already have before He gives you more. How well are you managing what you already have?

Matthew 25:23 His master replied, "Well done, good and faithful servant! You have been faithful with a few things; I will put you in charge of many things. Come and share your master's happiness!" (NIV)

One day you will stand before God and give an account of all that you have said and done. Imagine God looking you in the eye, saying, "Well done, good and faithful servant!" What decisions are you making today that will bear eternal fruit?

Notes:

Proverbs 13:4 The sluggard craves and gets nothing, but the desires of the diligent are fully satisfied. (NIV)

There is no doubt about it. Giving your best in life will take you a long way in satisfying your desires. God is like that! What word best describes you lately—sluggard or diligent?

Colossians 3:23,24 Work hard and cheerfully at whatever you do, as though you were working for the Lord rather than for people. Remember that the Lord will give you an inheritance as your reward, and the Master you are serving is Christ. (NLT)

You work for God Himself. He pays well and the retirement package is out of this world. How are you doing in your job serving the Lord?

Galatians 5:7 You were running a good race. Who cut in on you and kept you from obeying the truth? (NIV)

Don't let anything stop you from running the race that ends in God's loving arms. How is your race going?

Philippians 2:12,13 Continue to work out your salvation with fear and trembling, for it is God who works in you to will and to act according to his good purpose. (NIV)

Growth in any area of life requires effort. If you want to grow spiritually, then work at it. But do so knowing that it is God who is working in you. How would you describe your spiritual growth?

Notes:

Proverbs 16:24 Pleasant words are a honeycomb, sweet to the soul and healing to the bones. (NIV)

Today you have a chance to bring healing and hope to people in your life—some of whom may be dying inside. Text, email, or write some pleasant words to at least one person today. Who will that be and what sweet words can you use?

1 Thessalonians 5:15 Make sure that nobody pays back wrong for wrong, but always try to be kind to each other and to everyone else. (NIV)

If someone pokes you, you poke them back. Someone talks negatively behind your back, you talk negatively behind their back. Someone takes advantage of you, you... (You see the pattern). There is another way: kindness. Who in your life deserves a pay back that you can, instead, give kindness to?

1 Peter 4:10 God has given each of you a gift from his great variety of spiritual gifts. Use them well to serve one another. (NLT)

You are a gifted person. No, you don't think so? Well, it doesn't matter what you think. God says you are. What do you think your spiritual gift might be? How are you using it to be kind to others?

Philippians 2:4 Don't look out only for your own interests, but take an interest in others, too. (NLT)

Today find someone to listen to. Let them tell their story. Ask someone what they are excited about. You might just learn something. It might just get you out of a self-obsessed rut. Who can you listen to today?

Notes:

Proverbs 12:18 Reckless words pierce like a sword, but the tongue of the wise brings healing. (NIV)

The negative, unkind words you say to people or about people can hurt deeply. The positive, kind words you say to people or about people can heal deeply. Today, say something kind. In your own life, how have other people's kind words affected you?

1 Peter 3:9 Don't repay evil for evil. Don't retaliate with insults when people insult you. Instead, pay them back with a blessing. That is what God has called you to do, and he will bless you for it. (NLT)

You have been chosen to receive a blessing from God today. How do you get this blessing? Be kind to those who curse you. Don't believe it will work? Try it. Perhaps you will be surprised. Who has been handing out unkind words to you lately? How will you respond?

Colossians 3:12 Therefore, as God's chosen people, holy and dearly loved, clothe yourselves with compassion, kindness, humility, gentleness and patience. (NIV)

Shoes? Check. Shirt? Check. Pants or skirt? Check. Socks? Check. Kindness???? Don't forget to put on kindness. What will kindness look like on you today?

Notes:

Exodus 23:2 Do not follow the crowd in doing wrong. (NIV)

Being a person of integrity means you have spiritual and moral principles that guide your life. There is always pressure to get you to compromise. Plan and live your life guided by God's will. What sorts of things does "the crowd" try to convince you to do? How do you respond?

Proverbs 10:9 The man of integrity walks securely, but he who takes crooked paths will be found out. (NIV)

Today you will be faced with a decision—do the right thing or do the thing that would be best for you in the short run. When in the past did you choose the easy way only to get burned by that decision later on?

Luke 16:12 If you have not been trustworthy with someone else's property, who will give you property of your own? (NIV)

All that you have—your possessions, your gifts and talents, the good fortune that has come your way... all of it has been given to you on loan. One day the Lender will want an accounting. How have you done with what you have been given?

Amos 5:24 But let justice roll on like a river, righteousness like a never-failing stream! (NIV)

Think of your life and times as a river of God's power and presence. His righteousness and justice touch this world through your life. When you act with integrity,

God's righteousness rolls on. Why is doing the right thing important in your life? How do you know what the right thing is?

Notes:

Psalm 51:10-12 Create in me a pure heart, O God, and renew a steadfast spirit within me. Do not cast me from your presence or take your Holy Spirit from me. Restore to me the joy of your salvation and grant me a willing spirit, to sustain me. (NIV)

When you do not walk with integrity, your spirit suffers. But God will not leave you. His Spirit will sustain you. When do you most feel the joy of your salvation?

1 Samuel 2:3 Do not keep talking so proudly or let your mouth speak such arrogance, for the LORD is a God who knows, and by him deeds are weighed. (NIV)

Speak less about what you do, and do more. No one likes a braggart. Let your deeds speak for themselves. When are you tempted to speak proudly?

1 Samuel 16:7 But the Lord said to Samuel, "Don't judge by his appearance or height, for I have rejected him. The Lord doesn't see things the way you see them. People judge by outward appearance, but the Lord looks at the heart." (NIV)

The first thing you notice about people is what they look like. The first thing God notices is their heart. How often do you judge people based on looks? What can you do to look at people the way God looks at you?

Notes:

Isaiah 9:2 The people walking in darkness have seen a great light; on those living in the land of the shadow of death a light has dawned. (NIV)

Perhaps there was a time in your life that you were walking in darkness. No purpose. No meaning. Brokenness. Selfishness. Stubbornness. Seeking your own agenda. But then the Christmas light of Jesus chased all these shadows away. Who do you know that is walking a dark path this holiday season? What can you do to give hope?

Isaiah 11:1 A shoot will come up from the stump of Jesse; from his roots a Branch will bear fruit. (NIV)

Jesse was the father of King David to whom God promised an Heir who would sit on the throne forever. But the people waited hundreds of years during which time this promise seemed impossible—until Jesus was born. How has Jesus brought life out of something that was all but dead in your life?

Micah 5:2 But you, O Bethlehem Ephrathah, are only a small village. Yet a ruler of Israel (Jesus) will come from you, one whose origins are from the distant past. (NLT)

At times you may feel as though you are not important. Remember that God loves you, and He will do amazing, sometimes unexpected, things with your life. When have you seen God do amazing things in your life?

Luke 2:1 In those days Caesar Augustus issued a decree that a census should be taken of the entire Roman world. (NIV)

Notes:

If you visit Rome today you can see a statue of Caesar Augustus—the great and powerful emperor of the Roman world 2,000 years ago. He had no idea that God was using him to bring about the greatest miracle the world had ever seen—God becoming man. How does knowing God's plans supersede man's plans make you feel?

Isaiah 7:14 Therefore the Lord himself will give you a sign: The virgin will conceive and give birth to a son, and will call him Immanuel. (NIV)

Life can be so hard that you lose hope in certain situations. And it may seem as if no one can help. The word "Immnauel" means "God with us." How does knowing that God is with us, or more to the point, God is with you, bring hope where hope was gone?

Luke 1:34 "How will this be," Mary asked the angel, "since I am a virgin?" (NIV)

God may be calling you to some special task. What excuses will you have? Finish this sentence: "How will this be, since I am ____________?"

Luke 1:37 For nothing is impossible with God. (NLT)

Not your problems. Not your pain. Not your past, present or future. "Nothing is impossible with God." What sorts of "impossible" things has God made possible in your life? How does this give you hope for your future?

Notes:

***Isaiah 9:6* For to us a child is born, to us a son is given ... and he will be called Wonderful Counselor, Mighty God, Everlasting Father, Prince of Peace. (NLT)**

If Jesus is the Prince of Peace and you are related to Him, what does that make you? Royalty. Live up to your heritage today. Where can you use your influence to bring peace into your relationships?

***Luke 1:28* The angel went to [Mary] and said, "Greetings, you who are highly favored! The Lord is with you." (NIV)**

You face many difficult situations in life. Perhaps you worry that you cannot see a solution to these difficulties. It may seem as if no one can help. You feel alone. Remember: "The Lord is with you." How does knowing this bring you peace in worrisome situations?

***Luke 1:45* Blessed is she who has believed that the Lord would fulfill his promises to her!" (NIV)**

Perhaps you worry about what God seems to be asking of you. Don't sweat it. Be at peace. He is the one that will accomplish whatever He may be asking of you. What has God been asking you to do lately?

***Luke 2:1* In those days Caesar Augustus issued a decree that a census should be taken of the entire Roman world. (NIV)**

It is called the Pax Romana (Roman peace) and it lasted 200 years—roughly from the birth of Jesus through the establishment of the early church. This period of peace throughout the Roman empire allowed the message of Christmas to freely spread all over the Western world. How can you spread the message of Christmas this season?

Luke 2:7 She wrapped Him in cloths and placed Him in a manger, because there was no room ... in the inn. (NIV)

There's a lot of pressure to have a "perfect" Christmas with great gifts, caroling, and family. Often that makes our actual Christmas a let-down. We forget the first Christmas was far from perfect... Mary had to give birth in a stable! What blessings from God can you find in your disappointments of the season?

Luke 2:28-30 Simeon took him (the baby Jesus) in his arms and praised God, saying: "Sovereign Lord, as you have promised, you may now dismiss your servant in peace. For my eyes have seen your salvation." (NIV)

When Jesus was 8 days old, a total stranger recognized that He would one day be the Savior. Where in your life do you need a Savior?

Luke 2:16 So they hurried off and found Mary and Joseph, and the baby, who was lying in the manger. (NIV)

When you finally find what you are looking for, you can be at peace. The shepherds found Jesus. How about you?

Notes:

Notes:

Luke 1:31 ***You (Mary) will conceive and give birth to a son, and you are to call him Jesus. (NIV)***

The name Jesus mean "Savior." Christmas is about a Savior being sent to save those who would believe in Him. Do you know the joy of knowing the Savior?

Luke 1:46-48 ***Mary responded, "Oh, how my soul praises the Lord. How my spirit rejoices in God my Savior! For he took notice of his lowly servant girl, and from now on all generations will call me blessed." (NLT)***

Not a part of the elite group? Not from the right side of the tracks? Not from a prominent, well-to-do family? God is not a respecter of your social class or standing. Rejoice! He can and wants to use you, just as you are. What do you think God is calling you to do this Christmas season?

Luke 2:5,6 ***He (Joseph) took with him Mary, his fiancée, who was now obviously pregnant. And while they were there, the time came for her baby to be born. (NLT)***

My guess is there was joy at your birth many years ago. But even if there wasn't, the birth of Jesus means your life can be one of joy. What has caused joy in your life lately?

Luke 2:9 ***And, lo, the angel of the Lord came upon them, and the glory of the Lord shone round about them: and they were sore afraid. (KJV)***

Fear at first. But then when they heard the message

their fear turned to joy. Your fear can turn to joy as well this Christmas season. What fears are robbing you of your joy?

Luke 2:15 When the angels had left them and gone into heaven, the shepherds said to one another, "Let's go to Bethlehem and see this thing that has happened, which the Lord has told us about." (NIV)

The shepherds joyfully went to Bethlehem to meet and know Jesus Christ. You can get to know Him too, through Bible reading and prayer. What would it have been like to be one of the shepherds that night?

Luke 2:17,18 When [the shepherds] had seen [Jesus], they spread the word concerning what had been told them about this child, and all who heard it were amazed at what the shepherds said to them. (NIV)

When something good happens to you, you tell others. You don't need all the answers. You just share what God has done. Whom are you sharing with?

Isaiah 35:1,2 Even the wilderness and desert will be glad in those days. The wasteland will rejoice and blossom with spring crocuses. Yes, there will be an abundance of flowers and singing and joy! (NLT)

Maybe your life is like a wasteland - nothing grows, nothing works. Isaiah predicted that the coming of Jesus would be like flowers blooming in the desert - even a desert like yours. Are you open to the joy that can come your way when you let Jesus into your life?

Notes:

Notes:

Matthew 1:23 The virgin will be with child and will give birth to a son, and they will call him Immanuel—which means, "God with us." (NIV)

This is the Christmas story—God with us. God with us when we are alone, when we are afraid, when we are discouraged, when we are feeling helpless, when we need a friend, when we need to be loved. How has God been with you this Christmas season?

Luke 1:49,50 For the Mighty One is holy, and he has done great things for me (Mary). He shows mercy from generation to generation to all who fear him. (NLT)

God's love is one of the few things that lasts from one generation to the next. Pass it along to your family and friends this Christmas season. What is your most significant Christmas memory?

1 John 4:9 In this the love of God was made manifest among us, that God sent his only Son into the world, so that we might live through him. (ESV)

This little verse speaks volumes about what Christmas is truly all about. It's more than buying gifts, going to parties, putting up decorations, singing carols, and eating good food. Have you accepted the gift of God's love—His Son—into your life?

1 John 3:5 But you know that he appeared so that he might take away our sins. (NIV)

Jesus Christ became a man so that He could experience what you feel. He knows your joys, your sorrows, your hopes, and your fears. He loves you, and He sacrificed Himself for you. How have you given your sins to Jesus Christ?

***Luke 2:18,19* And all who heard it were amazed at what the shepherds said to them. But Mary treasured up all these things and pondered them in her heart. (NIV)**

Sometimes we need to share God's love out loud. Sometimes we need to ponder it quietly in our hearts. Are you in a "sharing" or a "pondering" phase right now?

***John 1:14* The Word became flesh and made his dwelling among us. We have seen his glory, the glory of the One and Only who came from the Father, full of grace and truth. (NIV)**

Treat others with love and forgiveness as Jesus did, and they will see Jesus in you—God's love will be made flesh in you. What are you doing to show your relationship with Jesus to others?

***John 3:16* For God so loved the world that he gave his one and only Son, that whoever believes in him shall not perish but have eternal life. (NIV)**

Take out the words "the world" and put your own name in this verse. God the Father gave up His Son for you. What does that say about how much you are worth?

Notes:

Notes:

Luke 2:16 So they hurried off and found Mary and Joseph, and the baby, who was lying in the manger. (NIV)

The shepherds, though they had no idea what they were doing or what His birth was all about, sought out the Savior, Jesus, born in Bethlehem. How about you?

Matthew 5:14 You are the light of the world—like a city on a mountain, glowing in the night for all to see. (NLT)

The Christmas lights are still shining, bringing joy to your community. Let your light bring joy to those around you today. Where is your light shining? Who has noticed it?

Matthew 2:1 After Jesus was born in Bethlehem in Judea, during the time of King Herod, Magi from the east came to Jerusalem and asked, "Where is the one who has been born king of the Jews? We saw his star in the east and have come to worship him." (NIV)

So many are seeking something to worship, something that is worth worshiping, that is worth serving, that is worth following. What are you seeking?

Matthew 2:9,10 The star [the wisemen] had seen in the east went ahead of them until it stopped over the place where the child was. When they saw the star, they were overjoyed. (NIV)

How do you find your way in this world? Perhaps you need a sign. "Lord give me a sign that I may follow

You." Who or what has been the "star" in your life pointing you to a relationship with Jesus?

Notes:

Matthew 2:11 They entered the house and saw the child with his mother, Mary, and they bowed down and worshiped him. Then they opened their treasure chests and gave him gifts of gold, frankincense, and myrrh. (NLT)

Gold for a king. Myrrh, which was used by a priest—one who interceded on our behalf before the throne of God. Frankincense, a spice used on the dead body of a loved one. All three gifts pointed to who Jesus is and what He came to do. Are you seeking Jesus this Christmas season?

Numbers 24:17 What I saw in my vision hasn't happened yet. But someday, a king of Israel will appear like a star. (CEV)

Maybe your vision for a bright future in this new year seems blurred. This year, look to the Star of Bethlehem—the secret to clear vision. What positive things do you see coming in this next year?

Philippians 3:13,14 ... One thing I do: Forgetting what is behind and straining toward what is ahead, I press on toward the goal to win the prize .... (NIV)

Taking hold. Straining toward. Pressing on. Goal. Win. Prize. What are you taking hold of? What are you straining toward? What is your goal? What do you want to win? Will you gain the prize?